How to Become a Heroic Writer

Train Your Brain to

Improve Habits, Overcome Obstacles, and

Reach Readers

JERRY WAXLER

How to Become a Heroic Writer by Jerry Waxler

First published in 2005 as *Four Elements for Writers* by Jerry Waxler

Copyright Second Edition 2014

Published by Neuralcoach Press

PO Box 99

Quakertown, PA 18951

www.neuralcoach.com

Cover Design: Maciej Krzywicki

Book Design: Karin Rex

Printed in the U.S.A.

10 9 8 7 6 5 4 3 2 1

ISBN 978-0-9771895-5-7

TABLE OF CONTENTS

PREFACE

This book is dedicated to those who wish to take the journey from "I love to write" to "I am a writer." Most guidebooks on this subject teach you how to improve literary skills or how to find readers. I wrote *How to Become a Heroic Writer* to help you manage your mind.

To become writers, we must maintain enthusiasm, reach tenaciously toward goals, applaud the steps we have taken so far, and plan the steps we will take next. Since the dawn of civilization, every culture has admired heroes who possess such psychological skills. To join their ranks, we attempt to acquire these traits for ourselves.

In moments of weakness, we worry that we lack these qualities, that we weren't born with courage, and that our lofty goals are out of reach. In moments of strength, we reach out to find support systems that will assist us on the journey of becoming writers.

Fortunately, such systems were built into the Western psyche by one of the architects of modern democracy. In his autobiography, Ben Franklin explained how he developed his character. His methods inspired many in subsequent generations who evolved ever more sophisticated systems of self-improvement.

By the end of the twentieth century, anyone who wanted to grow could choose from a rich, mature set of instructions for working their own minds. Over the final decades of that century, scientists became increasingly engaged in improving human nature. By the beginning of the twenty-first century, revolutionary discoveries turned their general interest into specific, focused research. Psychologists, neuroscientists and medical professionals teamed up to reveal the secrets of the growing brain.

How to Become a Heroic Writer collects this advice into an updated guidebook. These practical, modern techniques will empower you to enter a flow-state, overcome self-doubts and other drags on creativity, find time, and maintain courage so you can create writing that your readers will love.

Science and Wisdom

FOUR DECADES TO FIND THE WRITER'S WHOLE BRAIN

While I attended high school during the 1960s, I worked part-time at a research lab at Temple University's medical school. After scrubbing the day's accumulation of bloody beakers and test tubes, I used my spare time to learn how my body works. Sitting in the library, I read textbooks about the function of my lungs, kidneys, heart, and skin. Even my nervous system revealed beauty and purpose in its cascading flow of molecules across synapses. My boss, a physician, generously answered questions to help me put it all together.

He couldn't, however, explain the hundreds of parts of my brain. The more I read about these parts, the more fragmented I felt. How could I graduate high school without understanding my own mind? I turned to the writings of Sigmund Freud, the father of psychiatry. He described consciousness as a tiny island floating on the vast, dangerous ocean of the unconscious. According to him, we are at the mercy of mental forces beyond our control. I found his images unsettling.

By the time I entered college, I knew far more about my body than about my mind. College courses enlightened me about the physical universe, but when I completed my degree in physics, I had not yet learned how to become an effective person.

For the next forty years, I filled in the missing pieces of my self-understanding. I turned to self-help books, which taught me how to become more aware, satisfied, and engaged. After I studied each method, I attempted to apply it, learning how it worked for me, and discarding the parts that didn't help. Year after year, I applied technique after technique, and gradually I built up a repertoire of life skills.

When I conducted these experiments, I was not alone. My efforts paralleled the evolving self-development movement. Our entire culture was pushing for change. The books that I bought were bestsellers, and the methods they were giving me were at the same time being studied by millions of others. We were discovering together that adults can grow and change along lines of their choosing.

Through this lengthy project, I had participated in a fascinating, informative, modern self-help movement. Now it was my turn to extract the lessons I had learned and pass them to the next generation.

Right Brain: Decade of Free-writing and Journaling

Starting in the early 1970s, I sat at the local diner for an hour a day and poured my thoughts and feelings onto the pages of a journal. I rarely went back to reread what I had written earlier, and had no interest in publishing anything. But each session made me feel good, and I looked forward to doing it again. After years of this practice, I realized I had gained the knack of pouring out whatever came to mind, demonstrating that Freud was wrong about the scary unconscious. The words that emerged from these deep places made me feel whole.

Thanks to inspirational books such as Natalie Goldberg's *Writing Down the Bones*, and Julia Cameron's *The Artist's Way,* millions of us learned how to increase self-awareness through the simple act of writing. By teaching us how to bypass analytical thinking, these authors helped us get in touch with the currents of creativity flowing just beneath the surface.

During this surging interest in the creative power of the unconscious mind, artists and writers tapped into research that suggested that the two halves of the brain serve different purposes. The left half controls analytical thinking and the right half controls flow. By localizing different types of thinking to different sides, these teachers transformed the popular conception of the brain from a mysterious blob to an organ that made sense. My teenage desire for a map of the brain was beginning to materialize.

Left Brain: Decade of Self-development

Free-writing in a journal satisfied me, but because my journal entries rambled from one mental snapshot to another, I doubted they would ever make sense to readers. To improve my skills, I studied books about the craft of writing.

Reading these books was easy. Implementing their suggestions, though, required concentration. I could no longer sit at the local diner with pen and paper and scribble whatever came to mind. Sessions grew more difficult, and skipping them grew easier. Days slipped by with no writing at all, and then days turned into weeks. I felt trapped, no longer satisfied to write for myself, but unable to find the time or willpower to write in a structured style.

Speaking with a friend one day early in the 1980s, I told him my problem. "I can never find the time to write. Because he was a business owner, I assumed he would respond with a polite nod or roll of the eyes. Instead, he leaned forward with great interest and said, "Everyone has that problem. To achieve goals, you have to manage your priorities."

"You're kidding, right? This is writing. I can't treat it like a business."

"Of course you can. How else are you going to get anything done?"

He loaned me a shopping bag full of self-help tapes. During my commute, I listened to their enthusiastic, informative suggestions about working my mind. and learned about branches of the self-development movement I didn't even know existed. Their advice gradually helped me fit writing into my day, and won me over to the importance of applying analytical thinking to solve my creative problems.

The book that influenced me most was Stephen Covey's *Seven Habits of Highly Effective People*, which helped me apply the same effort to my personal goals as I would apply to my career. To succeed as a writer, I needed to apply effort and follow a plan. Above all, Covey convinced me that habits were an important component of a productive life, not only in business but in creative goals, as well. By forming a habit, I would create a pocket in time within which my creativity would flourish.

Since I didn't know how to start a habit, I read a book on the subject, *Changing for Good*, in which scientist-author James Prochaska analyzed the process of forming habits. By following his step-by-step advice, I established the habit of writing every day. During my daily session, I free-wrote first drafts and then kept going, editing and shaping them for readers.

Bottom Brain: Decade of Emotional Intelligence

So far, I had learned how the right and left sides of my brain could work together to help me craft words on the page. But when I imagined sharing my writing with strangers, I panicked. *What if they don't like it? What if they reject me?* The potential for criticism or disinterest terrified me. How could I write with conviction and enthusiasm if I was afraid of readers?

Because my overreaction was at times severe, I sought help. Therapy shed light on my insecurities and fears. Throughout the 1990s, I spoke to a therapist who listened while I rambled through my mind. He served as an audience for my introspection, and by inviting me to speak to him, he taught me that I didn't need to be alone with my thoughts.

During that period, I consumed a steady diet of self-help books. One book, *Emotional Intelligence* by Dan Goleman, taught me how my mid-brain, or *limbic system*, triggered my mind into emergency mode, shutting off the clear thinking at the top of the brain and stimulating the ancient survival systems at the bottom.

Goleman's insight into the brain provided me with new ways to understand my moods. When I felt the irrational fear that readers might hate me, I pictured my amygdala, triggering a fight-or-flight response. I knew fear would help me run faster if I were being chased by a predator, but the reaction did nothing to help me write. To counteract these irrational reactions, I learned how to encourage my brain to move back into balance.

One of the most valuable methods was Cognitive Therapy, which provided detailed instructions to help me improve my thoughts. I also learned to relax muscles and visualize positive images. Gradually the work paid off, helping me manage my emotions and connect with other people.

I became so interested in methods to manage my mind that I attended graduate school to learn how to be a talk therapist myself. By studying such methods as Cognitive Therapy and Neurolinguistic Programming (NLP), modern mental health technologies began to make sense.

After earning my master's degree, I began to write articles about what I learned. I took classes and joined groups, gaining insight into the craft, and at the same time, meeting other writers. When we talked about challenges of writing, I discovered that many of them shared similar problems such as shyness, low productivity, or self-doubt. Since I had spent decades figuring out how to solve these problems, I wished I could explain my findings. But teaching a workshop seemed impossible: All the fears I felt about writing were amplified a thousand-fold when I stood in front of a room and tried to speak.

To overcome my fear of public speaking, I attended Toastmasters International. My quaking knees and dry mouth convinced me I would never succeed. I stuck with it, and by diligently following the instructions and applying psychological techniques to quell my fear, those frightening audience members began to feel like friends.

Finally prepared to teach, I arranged a workshops. We sent out promotional material to members of the writing group and soon I was standing in front of a room filled with writers who wanted to overcome blocks and achieve their goals. By teaching the class, I learned even more about what fuels writers and what slows them down.

One of the most important lessons came not from the material but from the group experience itself. In a room full of writers, each one of us felt support from the others. Over the years, I learned that critique groups, workshops, clubs, forums, and conferences transform writing from an isolated activity, to a social one.

Top Brain: Decade of the Story

Talking to a therapist throughout the '90s taught me to piece together the events in my early life. Despite years of telling him about my past, it never occurred to me that anyone other than my therapist would be interested in my story. That changed in the early 2000s. I had been writing a self-help column for a local newspaper. To improve my articles, I asked *New York Times* bestselling author Jonathan Maberry to give me advice. He read my piece and said, "It sounds like your ideas are falling from the sky. You need to include more of yourself." My first reaction was dismay. *Oh, no! I have no idea how to write about myself. I have to learn another skill.*

I realized Jonathan had highlighted an important weakness in my personal toolkit. I had not yet learned how to share myself with others. The advice to "include more of myself" did more than improve my writing. It also built bridges that helped me relate to strangers. Jonathan's apparently simple suggestion opened up a new chapter in my writing life.

The determination to find a story within my life turned into a passion. I dug deeper into lifestory writing, and discovered Joseph Campbell's pioneering study of mythology, *Man With a Thousand Faces.* Campbell points out similarities among tribes all over the world. Building on Campbell's ideas, Brian Boyd's *On the Origin of Stories* theorized that humans evolved the powerful *neocortex* at the top of the brain in order to tell stories.

Continued research showed me that stories are far more important than simple entertainment. Each of us relies on the story of ourselves to provide a roadmap for our actions, feelings, and dreams. We construct a self-image over a period of years, absorbing the influence of parents, extended family, siblings, teachers, books, traumas, successes, the news media, our friends, and so on.

Our stories-of-self are also influenced by the stories we hear. For example, the Grimm Fairy Tale *Little Red Riding Hood* teaches children social fundamentals such as wariness about people who create false self-images. Many of the stories we hear teach us to become the best versions of ourselves. We admire heroes who courageously fight for what they know is right. By applying that model to our own lives, we grow wiser and braver, too.

In my workshops, I showed aspiring writers how to use stories as self-help tools. By casting themselves in the roles of hero-writer, they could move toward goals, increase skills, and tenaciously maintain momentum. Crafting their self-images helped them acquire the emotions, the motivations, and the actions of being writers.

The storytelling part of your brain integrates and directs the other parts. Becoming the storyteller of your own aspirations carries you through difficult as well as exciting times, and helps you overcome obstacles on your journey.

SCIENTIFIC REVOLUTION: YOUR BRAIN CAN GROW!

At the beginning of the twenty-first century, I was onstage at a writers' conference. Just as I was explaining how aspiring writers can gain psychological skills, a commotion in the back of the large amphitheater-style classroom distracted me. Someone appeared to be shouting at me. I tried to make sense of what the well-dressed, gray-haired man was saying.

"Some people just don't have the talent. They shouldn't even try to write." He spoke angrily, as if he felt insulted by every untalented person who picked up a pen. His arrogance infuriated me. This is exactly the type of wounding insinuation that blocks many would-be writers. *How dare he sow such doubts in my workshop! And why is he wearing a suit and tie?*

My mind raced, trying to undo his humiliating pronouncement. I knew from personal experience that one *can* develop the literary and psychological skills necessary for becoming a writer. But scientific dogma directly contradicted my observations. For decades, almost all brain scientists believed that adult brains are in a constant state of deterioration. These scientific observations supported this man's cynical claim that if you weren't born with talent, there's no point in trying to acquire it.

With the moments ticking by and the rest of my audience suspended, waiting to learn how to become writers, I finally muttered that I disagreed. I continued teaching, frustrated by the interaction, and fascinated to discover that it is possible to be heckled during a writing workshop.

At that very moment, however, in labs around the world, scientists were dismantling the doctrine upon which this man based his prejudice. In experiment after experiment, researchers discovered that when we attempt to change our minds, our neurons adapt accordingly. This simple fact that effort changes your brain offers revolutionary potential for adults who want to write.

COMPLETING THE WISDOM REVOLUTION

Ben Franklin, in addition to being one of the masterminds of the Declaration of Independence, and an architect of a democratic nation, also happened to be a best-selling author. One of his most influential books was his autobiography, in which he provided detailed instructions about how he improved his character. Ben Franklin never suggested it was easy to change, but through tenacious effort, he demonstrated that it was possible. His instructions, offered in quaint, antiquated language, provided a legacy that offered hope for personal improvement.

Two hundred years later, Americans continued to accept the idea that in order to be upwardly mobile in a free economy, they needed to improve themselves psychologically. Modern variations of Franklin's suggestion for self-development continued to dominate bestseller lists. For example, Norman Vincent Peale's *Power of Positive Thinking* taught millions of people how to improve their lives by changing their thoughts. In the final decades of the twentieth century, psychologists provided a scientific basis and methodology to these popular ideas.

Over the centuries, hundreds of millions of people around the world have attempted to follow the fundamental idea Ben Franklin proposed, that in order to achieve our dreams we could improve personal characteristics. No matter how much evidence the psychologists amassed, however, many scientists continued to believe that self-development is biologically impossible. They said that since the brain can't grow, self-development is nothing more than wishful thinking.

The brain scientists turned out to be wrong. Images of the brain showed that when adults attempted to learn, their brain cells grew accordingly. Based on this discovery, scientists turned their attention from debunking self-development, to improving it.

The discovery of *neuroplasticity*, that is, the ability to grow and change our neurons through directed effort, spawned a revolution in brain exercise and self-development. Inspired by that wave, Martin Seligman, former president of the prestigious American Psychological Association, broadened the emphasis of the profession beyond its original goal of curing disease. The movement he dubbed *Positive Psychology* guides people to maximize their strengths, resilience, and happiness.

Thanks to the continued study of neuroplasticity, psychologists learned how to help people recover from stroke, maintain mental agility during aging, and assist school children with learning disabilities. Conditions that had previously been considered "hard wired" into the brain now became treatable. For example, Jeffrey Schwartz, M.D., coached patients with Obsessive Compulsive Disorder (OCD) to resist their compulsions. After they followed his instructions, images showed their brains had changed.

Schwartz's experiment validated Ben Franklin's assertion that you can change in response effort. This revolution does not provide freedom from kings and tyrants. Instead, it is directed against our own limitations.

In this modern atmosphere, fueled by the new science of neuroplasticity, writers are discovering their own voices. With the help of another modern technology, the Internet, writers can reach millions by typing on their computers and sending their words out to the world.

If you didn't think you would ever learn to write because your brain "doesn't work that way" or you assumed you could never overcome your self-doubts, *neuroplasticity* sets you free. The new science has ushered in a Golden Age of self-help.

Neuroplasticity supports Brenda Ueland, author of *If You Want to Write*. In 1938, she asserted that, "Everyone is talented, original and has something important to say." Neuroplasticity also supports author Julia Cameron's claim in *The Artist's Way* that those who think they have no talent are wounded artists, and by moving toward creativity, they will heal.

Today, after years of progress in neuroplasticity, if someone in one of my writing workshops said, "Some people shouldn't write," I would calmly respond, "The writing talent you have right now is simply your current best effort to communicate. Writers improve with practice, and brains grow accordingly. Through striving, you increase your talent along lines of your choosing."

Your Story as a Writer

THE STORY YOU TELL ABOUT YOURSELF

Imagine this story: Wherever you are right now in your life, you realize that something is missing. You have a desire to express yourself. You've always loved to write and want to develop a deeper relationship with the craft. So you read books about writing and then attend a conference. You look around at the other attendees and realize you are not alone.

You join a group of peers with whom you share your work. With regular effort, you polish one piece and fantasize about publishing it. This is the step you've been looking for – to move beyond writing for yourself, and cross the threshold into writing for readers.

This brings you face to face with a new challenge. You must learn how to reach them, so you study the *business* of writing. To achieve all of this, you must carve time out of your day. You make decisions about how to spend your time, and wrestle with the possibility that you're not good enough, or that this will never work. *What if no one likes it?* Now, in addition to good writing, you must find the courage to send it out.

Finally you publish your piece. You've achieved another step toward your dream. Next, you have to do it again. Gradually you become accustomed to writing and publishing. One morning, as you sit at your computer preparing your next piece, or perhaps someone asks you what you did over the weekend, you realize you have become a writer.

That simple story is the narrative version of the life that you want to live. Every writer has followed a similar path. When you tell your own life journey as a story, you take advantage of the structure of stories you have been reading, watching, and hearing your whole life.

Here's the basic structure of a story. A character, in this case you, wants to achieve a goal. You move toward that goal by making effort. As you get closer, more obstacles appear, and you must overcome those obstacles. Then, finally, you achieve satisfaction.

As an aspiring writer, instead of merely receiving other people's stories, you now have an opportunity to craft your own. The stories you tell about yourself act as maps or guidelines that help you move to the next step. So as a writer, instead of passively living each day based on the unedited version of yourself, begin to shape a story that leads you to your dreams. As the purposeful hero of that story, you can surpass limitations, overcome resistance and discouragement, and live in harmony with your conscious goals. Developing a more positive story of yourself as a writer can boost your self-esteem, your resiliency, and your ability to publicly share your writing.

LET YOUR PAST PROPEL YOU

To start the process of shaping your story as a writer, look back across your journey so far. All sorts of details come to mind, such as where you lived and went to school, the key people in your life, and so on. At first the memories appear as a hodgepodge of details. To construct your story-of-self, you must organize them into a coherent whole. To do so, ask yourself questions about yourself, write the answers, and arrange them in chronological order.

WRITING PROMPT

> Start a computer file that contains the timeline of your life with headings of the years that are important to your story. At one writing session, list the key events during those years and place them on the timeline. At another session, describe the places where you lived. At another, describe the friends you knew during those years. Gradually the file will grow, and your past will become an "open book" that you can mine for valuable insights into your journey as a writer.

For example:

1966
Volunteered to work on school newspaper

1970
In Berkeley, tried to find writing groups, but was confused by my own intensity

1976
Started writing in a journal

1979
First job as a technical writer

1985
Wrote an essay for a newsletter

By writing the timeline of your past, you discover the accumulated choices, interactions, and relationships that created the person you are today. As the story comes together, instead of simply watching it unfold, become an active participant in its development. Delve into your past, respect it, and flow with it through the present and into the future. Find points in it where you saw or didn't see yourself as a writer, and when you learned your relationship to writing.

Heal Unproductive Patterns at Their Source

Suppose you believe that every sentence must be perfect before you can move to the next one. If you try to press on and write the next sentence before the first one is perfect, you feel that you have violated some sort of holy rule. To distance yourself from this or other unproductive rules that are slowing you down, it helps to understand how you established the pattern. What were you thinking? Why is this so important to you?

Talk therapy is an effective tool to help you untangle the causes of your personal rulebook. By talking about the way you arrived at the rule, you can reevaluate whether or not you want to continue following it.

In addition to talk therapy, writers have access to another powerful tool to understand the sequence of earlier decisions. By organizing your journey into a story, you can discover the source of self-limiting habits that slow you down, and discover options to help you move forward more productively.

For example, to understand the source of distorted ideas about perfectionism, look at the way you learned about mistakes. When your teachers corrected you, their disapproval hurt. Your parents may have added to the problem by criticizing small linguistic infractions, convincing you that their love for you depended on your perfect language skills. The fear of disapproval that started in childhood lingers. As a result, you might hate all critical thinking about your words, and even the possibility of criticism drains the pleasure out of writing.

By writing the story of your own journey, you can reach back into those memories and offer yourself compassion and praise. That child needed love specifically related to writing and communicating. Pour on the love, and soothe the anxiety.

> *Note: To further pursue the healing of your inner writer, follow Julia Cameron's workbook,* The Artist's Way. *Her daily writing method and encouraging words help you get in touch with the love and appreciation you deserve.*

Transform Regrets into Steps on Your Path

When I was a hippie in California, I made an effort to become a writer. I wrote an article for UC Berkeley's student newspaper, which the editor published without changing.

What a rush! I enjoyed writing, and enjoyed seeing my name in print. Thrilled with myself, I wrote another one. The editor thought it was great and wanted to print it, but at the last minute, I pulled it away. Even though she liked it, I was afraid it wasn't good enough. I slunk away, unsure of what to do with my fears. I wrote poetry and felt that exhilaration of seeing my thoughts and feelings emerge on the page. Then I showed it to a group of writers. Their suggestions for improving the piece hurt my feelings. I thought they ought to adore my piece not criticize it. I withdrew from the group and began storing my writing in a cardboard box. When I moved east, I threw out the box, certain I could never be a writer.

Those experiences represent turning points in my life. With more courage, I might have been able to accept the danger of criticism, and keep growing as a writer. Instead, I threw that opportunity away. Now, I must make another choice. If I regret the past, it could become a bitter reminder of the way life might have been. Or with more courage, I could look at those decisions as the mistakes of a young man who needed to find his way.

Writing about painful memories might at first appear to be dangerous and foolhardy, but this creative effort produces a paradoxical effect. By writing about earlier choices, you can contain them in words, organize them on paper, and become their author. Upsetting setbacks and humiliations, turn into interesting – even entertaining – slices of life.

Story-writing reveals its real power when individual scenes weave together into a narrative. You can watch yourself unfold, transitioning from one segment of your life when you were sure you wanted to do one thing, to another period with different desires and rules. Gradually you appreciate the length and complexity of this journey and realize it as an epic tale in which you grow and change.

When you turn life into a story, the passage of time and the courage of the main character sweep you through difficulties. A memory that originally caused suffering becomes a step along the path to acceptance, self-improvement and eventual victory. Your own story will show how each event leads to the next. At each stage, you had the opportunity to renew your enthusiasm and fulfill your potential. With conscious attention and planning, you can rise above failings of the past and build patterns that lead you toward success. By applying the story model to your life, you exchange regret for hope.

In your story, you see the forces that influenced you. You were young. You couldn't see the future. You had to figure out so much about life and had so little wisdom to guide you. By using your own words, you develop a layer of knowledge about yourself that lifts you above the helplessness engendered by memory alone.

The way you look at your memories can profoundly influence your writing energy today. If you try to forget the past, it lingers in its original form, ready to pounce from the shadows. Use storytelling to transform residual regrets from anchors that drag you down, into dramatic tension that propels you forward.

By writing your own story, you can come to understand and even admire your journey. Within your story, you discover that regrets are side effects of your desire to grow. You learn to nurture the desire instead of dwelling on the failures. Celebrate that part of you that wants to be a more energetic, better-informed writer. In fact, by focusing on this creative desire, you can quickly bounce back to the joy of writing.

WRITING PROMPT

What choices about writing do you regret, for example, sabotaging an educational opportunity or not being courageous enough to attempt a change? Since you can't turn the clock back, try to capture the sequence in a short story, and let the forward momentum of the story create a positive flow.

Write a scene before the regrettable event. Remember your hope and excitement. After the bad decision, the desire lingered under the surface. What small or large acts did you do to keep it alive? Months or years later, a new opportunity presented itself. This time you are older, wiser, and ready to embrace the opportunity.

Fiction-writing alternative: Substitute a fictitious regret for a real one. For example, suppose I had become a successful writer and then discovered I lacked the emotional maturity to handle success, so I turned to booze. By turning my regrets into a sequence that could have been much worse, my actual journey doesn't seem so bad after all.

Memory with Dignity. Be Kind to Your Younger Self

Letting go of regret doesn't mean deleting events from memory and only keeping good ones. Both good and bad experiences are threads in the rich tapestry of your life. You wouldn't be you without them. You survived and continued to struggle another day. The hero of any engaging story faces a variety of serious obstacles. In fact, a story without obstacles is hardly a story at all. Instead of trying to lift your mood by forgetting unpleasant memories, use your story-telling imagination to turn them into growth or enrichment opportunities. Your courage and resiliency made you a stronger, more interesting character.

WRITING PROMPT

Continue writing and layering your story of becoming a writer, focusing as much as possible on your compassion for your younger you. Write about this younger person. You were immature and your choices were a normal outcome of who you were at the time. Glorify your earlier decision and recognize it as a sort of wisdom, in which the younger-you knew there were other roads to follow first. Pour compassion, forgiveness, and acceptance onto this younger version of yourself. Look back at those events as steps along the road to success. Write the story of these events from this forgiving perspective. Celebrate the messy process of being young, and learning how to live.

By seeing your trials and setbacks as a valid part of a healthy life, you will gain a new sense of power over these events, and change them from mistakes into important stepping stones.

Break the Spell of Obsolete Decisions

After I backed away from my initial attempts to become a writer in my early twenties, I assumed the opportunity had passed. *I don't have the skill or the heart. I'm too sensitive to criticism and can't handle the possibility that my writing won't be loved. The writing life isn't going to work for me. It spit me out.* My evaluation of my relationship to writing seemed so final, so true. After a few years I added new reasons for not being a writer. I was too old to start, and since I was no longer drowning in the turbulent emotions of my youth, I didn't have much to write about, anyway. Despite all my reasons not to write, I continued to feel the nagging desire to express myself.

After years of writing only for myself, and then more years as a technical writer, I decided to look back at some of the decisions I made in those stormy years just after college. I realized that the failure back then was not related to my skill as a writer, but to my emotional ability to handle feedback. To write for others, I would need new emotional skills. By this time in my life, I had learned quite a bit about my own emotions, and felt ready to tackle these challenges. But the first step was to revise my decision that "I would never be a writer" and replace it with the willingness and commitment to try.

If you feel limited in your writing life today because of decisions you made years ago, take another look. Consider the pressures you were under back then and feel empathy for your younger self. Even if you wish your circumstances and choices had been different, soften your harsh judgment against your past. You did what you thought you had to do at the time. Since then, your circumstances have changed. The former choice was simply a step on a longer path. Now you choose to return from your detour and continue where you left off.

For example, a mother stopped writing in order to start a family. Looking back, she acknowledges it was the right decision for the time. Now to move forward, she consciously revises her internal rulebook and gives herself permission to start writing again. Another woman followed her parents' advice to study law. That seemed like a practical, responsible thing to do. She can't change the decision she made in the past, but she can revise it now and follow her own dream, to become a writer.

Perhaps in your younger years, you were hurt and confused by comments directed at you during a critique group, so you decided you would never let anyone see your work again. You can't change how you felt back then. But now you decide to override your fear of feeling agitated, knowing that by tolerating those emotions, you will improve your skill.

By introducing hope into the story of you as a writer, you expand your possibilities. Hope acknowledges that after things descend, they rise again, like the flowers at the end of the winter. Bask in the sunshine of new possibilities.

WRITING PROMPT

> Remember a time when you decided writing wasn't working.
> Perhaps after a rejection you decided you weren't "good enough,"
> or that writing wasn't worth the anxiety. Describe those
> circumstances and feelings. Then, write a letter to yourself,
> addressing it to the person you were when you made the decision.
> In your letter, empathize with the pressures that created the
> earlier decision, respect that it made sense at the time, and explain
> that you are now ready to make a new decision, to renew your
> hope, and turn toward writing.

Mine Memories for Positive States of Mind

Actors generate authentic joy, tears, or anger by imagining themselves in emotionally charged episodes in their lives. You can follow their example and use your own memories to influence your current mood.

If you need pride and confidence today, review your past for those emotions. Perhaps you experienced a surge of pride and confidence when you were elected to a school office, starred in a school play, or won a sporting event. By allowing yourself back into that experience, you can evoke that state of mind today. To feel playful, remember your state of mind when playing a game. To feel tenacious, remember a time when you persisted despite setbacks. To feel the power of study, remember a time when you needed to learn a skill, researched it, practiced, and then improved.

Writing scenes gives you emotional "ownership" of your own experience. Even though the actual experience ended long ago, writing it as a scene engages similar emotions. Here is an example of a scene from my past:

> When I was 16, my biology teacher told us that during summer break we should learn about the structure of DNA. To motivate us, he ranted about how young people could never understand the importance of study. I decided to prove him wrong.
>
> I remember the thick, glossy pages of my beloved *Scientific American*, showing the beautiful double-spiral of the DNA molecule, made up of sequences of nucleotides. Their names rolled off my tongue like poetry: adenine, guanine, thymine, and cytosine, or A, G, T, and C for short. This was the alphabet of life, and its sequence determined if I had blue eyes or green, or for that matter if I was a baboon, a squid, or a boy.
>
> I drank in the simplicity and power of nature's design as described by scientists. I wanted to know it all! It was my cry to the universe, and every morsel, every neuron, every breath pressed to the challenge. These coded spirals felt as beautiful and important as anything I had yet learned. I felt as if I were sprinting up the mountain of knowledge, following the giants who would reveal insights not only into the world, but the whole universe. I was ready for knowledge. Bring me more!

My excitement took place during my coming-of-age when I thirsted to understand the world. At the same time, I happened to have a zealous biology teacher who pushed me to my intellectual limits. This intense period is in the distant past, and yet the feelings echo in my imagination and even in my body.

Peak moments lift our spirits to fabulous heights and then gradually fade into the recesses of memory. To unearth these treasures, consciously scrape away the layers of forgetfulness. As you explore the narrative of your past, perhaps you will remember a successful project at work, school, or play. List milestones and transitions such as graduations, new beginnings, and big moves. Transcendent moments might have come while listening to music or gazing at the ocean.

WRITING PROMPT

> Describe scenes when you felt lifted into the positive states of a writer. For example, "wrote a poem in Berkeley 1969," and "published an article in the student paper." Surround each instance of self-confidence with a few details, like when it happened, or whom you were with. When one of these events starts to come alive in your memory, write the scene. Describe sensory detail, such as sights, sounds, smells and textures. Become aware of body sensations, such as breathing deeply, or a sensation of lightness. Were your shoulders relaxed and erect, your vision open to the whole world?

WRITING PROMPT

> Expand your search to include other deep learning experiences, such as when you learned a sport, craft, musical instrument, or skill. Focus on one of these learning experiences. Rewind to the very beginning, before you knew how to do it. Then list the sources of your new knowledge, such as teachers, books, or practice. Visualize a moment when you felt a breakthrough, and another when you felt proficient. Think of a particular scene that represents your willingness to overcome obstacles, stop listing the events, and on a clean sheet start writing the scene.

By returning to times when you felt curious, energetic, creative, or empowered, you will awaken those feelings.

- You feel the thrill of communicating with an appreciative or curious friend.

- You rapidly select fun words or ideas from the cornucopia flowing through your mind.

- You effortlessly ignore distractions, and pull your attention away from extraneous thoughts to focus on your project.

- You start from ignorance, and then add knowledge, skill, and practice until you achieve competence.

Develop a repertoire of such memories, flesh them out, and incorporate them as important elements of yourself. Then use these feelings to conquer obstacles, on the journey toward your dreams.

Review Your Past to Foster Wisdom

Many of your past decisions led you in effective and satisfying directions. For example, you decided to work hard. As a result, you created a home, family, and career. When you review the sequence of events in your autobiography, you can see how your actions added up. In retrospect, you see that it took years for your effort to bear fruit. By seeing the way effort accumulated in the past you can project forward and see how today's positive steps will yield tomorrow's success. Autobiography provides appreciation for the long sweep of time, and reinforces the fact that your resolve to follow your writing dreams will continue to lead you on the writing journey.

WRITING PROMPT

> Scan your memory for decisions related to your writing. Write about the long-term results of these choices. Let your successes boost the confidence you feel about ongoing decisions to succeed.

Craft a story about how your current writing activities will affect you over the next few years.

FOLLOW THE STORY OF YOUR FUTURE

Rather than accepting whatever self-image your mind dishes up, you can apply the excitement of stories to consciously amplify the positive aspects and help you through rough spots. Consider what happens when you embark on a writing project. You start with the creative surge of an idea and the determination to turn it into a completed product. You look at the blank page, and then march into the world of your characters or information. You make progress. Then life distracts you. And then again, you forge ahead with determination. Exhilarated by success, you see the end in sight. Wait. You're not there yet. You receive an editorial comment that plunges you back into uncertainty. Finally you are filled with the joy of creative satisfaction.

Notice the motivation coursing through your fingers. Feel your courage when you overcome obstacles or cunningly sidestep them. Even as you complete your project, the story is not over yet. You peer into the future, and see how you will establish a relationship with your readers.

As the protagonist in this autobiography, give yourself the same determination and sense of destiny as you would expect from the hero of any good story. Visualize yourself pressing forward from project to project, learning techniques, and accumulating victories. During pauses, savor your accomplishments and draw strength from the gradual achievement of your goals.

WRITING PROMPT

Write a story about your current or next writing project. How will it feel to work on it? How long will it take? How will you solve the problems that stand in your way? What will it feel like to finish?

Apply Your Hero's Courage to Your Future

When attempting to visualize yourself as a character in a story, you will encounter the universal problem we all face when standing at the threshold between who we are and who we want to become. Changing your image requires courage.

Your self-image results from years of training and habit. If you have recently developed the aspiration to succeed as a writer, you may not have had time to reshape your internal story-of-self to match your new goals. In fact, you might even have the unconscious notion that a person like you is unlikely to succeed. You might think, "It's too late. There's not enough time." Or, "I didn't grow up writing, so I'll never be a real writer."

In order to change these unconscious assumptions, consciously and energetically cast yourself in the role of a writer. Inject courage and optimism to turn the future into an inviting story, with you as a hero-traveler who is overcoming obstacles on the journey and striving toward your dreams.

Every Hero Aims toward Goals

Daily writing inspires hope and improves clear-thinking, and journal writing can act as a form of meditation, bringing peace as you pour words onto the page. But when you feel the call to transition from writing for yourself to writing for readers, you must flex new muscles and learn new skills. You can develop the emotional strength you will need on this journey by following the example of your heroes.

By the time you're an adult, you have identified with the main character in thousands of stories. In comic books, television shows, movies and novels, the protagonist needed to achieve a goal, whether it was to win romance, solve a crime, or save the world. All these characters had to press through obstacles to achieve the resolution of the story.

In real life, too, you have been exposed to an endless procession of actual people who have strived for success. Your teachers at school, the authors of every book you read, the politicians who won office, the doctors who treat your illness, all had to overcome difficulties.

As an aspiring writer, you too have a purpose. Your future novel, movie, memoir, or poetry anthology defines the end point of your journey. When you hit a snag, you don't give up. You strive, learn skills, solve problems, and keep going. Your goal inspires you with hope, sustains your momentum, and replenishes your passion when you falter.

Describe Specific Outcomes

To reach for a goal, you need to define it. Aiming for specific goals can galvanize your attention and help you stay focused.

WRITING PROMPT

What accomplishment would fulfill your dreams? Describe in detail your goals for a specific period of time, say, the next three months. For example, "I want to finish a first draft of a book," or "I want to complete three polished articles and submit each one to a literary journal."

Once you know your larger goal, break it down into steps, and then strive to achieve each one. For example, you need to write a first draft. A first draft of what exactly? You try to write an overview or outline. The tasks of writing a draft and writing an outline require different aspects of your mind. Instead of bunching the two goals together, tease them apart, and focus on each one as a separate goal. When taken individually, it's easier to focus.

If you feel overwhelmed by a project, step back and work on smaller steps. Write a plan that will take you step by step toward your goal. As you attempt to move forward through this plan, some steps might require even closer consideration.

- If a step requires a particular writing skill, make a plan to sharpen that skill.

- If a step requires that you reach out to a person for assistance, build a plan to achieve that goal. Who are the people who can help? How can you improve your enthusiasm and clarity about making the connection?

- If you want to publish your work, what type of publication will be suitable? List specific publications that fit this description. If you're not sure how to find such publications, list several methods you can use to learn about such resources.

Use free-writing and brainstorming to convert generalized impressions into a specific writing flow. Attend workshops, talk to mentors and coaches, and do everything you can to understand where you are headed. I'll talk more about these methods in the *Act Like a Writer* section. By writing all these steps into your life story, you become a writer.

Aspire to a Variety of Goals

In addition to the goal of completing the written work itself, aim for the many other dimensions of the writing life. Here are some of the rewards to move toward:

ALTER YOUR STATE OF MIND

Just as readers can suspend disbelief and hypnotically enter into a novel, writers experience a sense of immersion in the pieces they write. Like the endorphin high that marathon runners report during a long run, writers who immerse themselves in a project can enter into a pleasurable state of mind that they have created through their words.

DEEPEN YOUR IDENTITY AS A WRITER

The more you write, the easier it is to visualize yourself as a writer. As you become a writer, your acquire a sense of identity that includes a creative role and purpose.

IMPROVE LANGUAGE AND STORY ARTS

By writing regularly and striving to become more skillful, you improve your mastery of the artful, effective use of language.

CONTRIBUTE TO CULTURAL DIALOGUE

Throughout your life, you have been receiving cultural creativity produced by others. When you start publishing, you contribute your own creativity into that dialogue.

TEACH

After years of learning, you want to pass your knowledge to others. Publishing gives you the opportunity to give back.

RECOGNITION AND CREDENTIALS AS AN EXPERT

When you become fascinated by a field and]research it, eventually you will amass enough knowledge and insight into the field to begin to add to the public conversation. Your publications, over time, establish your reputation as a knowledgeable commentator or even contributor to the field. The reputation you establish through writing becomes a credential that can help you with your other work, such as teaching, coaching, or public speaking.

IMPROVED SOCIAL CONNECTIONS

Many writers are introspective or even shy. By writing for others to read, your words offer another channel through which to relate. Of course, written stories and ideas don't replace personal social connections, but written words can certainly enhance the mutual understanding that binds us to each other.

Money

I once attended a seminar for professional sales people. The instructor asked a question and then, holding out a dollar, said "This goes to the first person who answers." The audience erupted in a hubbub of enthusiasm. These people were accustomed to motivating themselves with money, and even a tiny amount focused enormous amounts of attention. You, too, might be able to take advantage of the motivating power of money by dangling financial rewards in your future.

I know of one writer who bribes himself with a reward at the end of each successful deadline. Obviously the technique requires a bit of self-trickery. He could give himself the reward anytime he wants. But he has chosen to manage his mind in order to focus his attention.

A more practical use of money would be to look forward to earning a fee for an article, book, or movie script. Even a small payment for an article could validate your hard work and talent. As a beginning writer, financial rewards wait for you in the future. Initially the promise for money will remain a figment of your imagination. By maintaining that image, you might be able to fuel your motivation in the present.

Too much focus on what's in it for you, could cloud your vision and make you forget that your readers are asking the same question. Every time they decide whether or not to read your writing, they want to know what they will gain. To earn their respect, be sure to focus at least as much energy on what you give, as on what you receive. When you generously give yourself to your readers, you will earn their trust, and eventually their money.

For long-lasting success, introduce the element of patience. Your early non-paying audience could make important contributions to your creative identity. As you grow more skillful and mature, your prospects and reputation will grow, too.

WRITING BOOKS AND ARTICLES THAT AID YOUR BUSINESS

There are other ways writing can help you pay the bills. By writing articles and books, you give readers a reason to trust you, relate to you, and maintain business relationships with you.

PAID WRITING, EDITING, AND DAY JOBS

Another way to use writing to pay the bills is by incorporating your love for the craft into your day job. When you need to write a letter to a customer, describe a product, or write a report, slow down and focus on your words. Savor the act of achieving the best possible communication. You must use words appropriate to your task, and anticipate how those words will be perceived. No matter how mundane this use of language may seem, putting words into sentences in order to create an effect in a reader inches you closer to the very essence of the writing life.

I worked for years as a technical writer. It allowed me to earn a living doing something I loved, while contributing value to my family, coworkers and customers. When I met other technical writers, I realized I was in the company of people who earned a living by writing, a wonderful enhancement to the sense of "becoming a writer." Gradually, I increased the time I devoted to writing for personal satisfaction and gained the best of both worlds: a paycheck at the office and a creative expression at home.

Goals Evolve Over Time

As you reach toward your goals and overcome obstacles along the way, you grow wiser, which may in turn cause you to modify your goals. Take, for example, my journey. At each stage of life, I learned enough to move on to the next one.

When I was in my twenties and filled with the unlimited possibilities offered by creativity, I thought I could pour the jewels from my mind onto paper. These jewels, however, ended up in a cardboard box. I had no idea how to reach readers. As I entered my adult years, the realities of earning a living humbled me, and I turned my passion for writing into a career as a technical writer. Meanwhile, I continued to write for myself, feeling the pleasure of pouring words on the page but uncertain how to move to the next step.

During those years, my curiosity about people grew stronger. I wanted to learn how they thought, felt, and behaved. I earned a master's degree in Counseling Psychology when I was around 50. In order to actually counsel people, I began to realize I needed to reach out to them, so I overcame my fear of readers. I started a website and posted articles with prosaic titles like "Anxiety" and "Depression." I was beginning to shift my perspective about writing from "expressing myself" to "serving readers."

Searching for feedback to help me make my articles more meaningful, I joined a critique group. The other writers in the group didn't understand what I was trying to do. "These pieces aren't really articles. Are they brochures?" My fellow writers convinced me I needed to learn how to shape my writing into the structures that readers expect. I began writing essays about feeling better and living well. But I was still stuck. How could I write about psychology without making it sound like a textbook?

Through a combination of psychological insights during therapy and comments from readers during critique sessions, I discovered that I had spent my life trying to stay invisible and just write about my ideas. How could I, as a writer, ever expect to reach readers if, at the same time, I was trying to hide from them? This realization sent me on a journey to find my own story, a ten year quest that put me into the midst of a cultural fascination with life stories. I discovered that by learning to tell the story of my life, I could explain the things I learned along the way.

Every time I solved one puzzle, I found another. I saw higher up the mountain, and kept climbing. It all added up over time.

WRITING PROMPT

> To understand the way your own goals change over time, look back over the years of your writing ambition. List milestones, starting from your first glimmer of hope or frustration about wanting to write. By reviewing the things you wanted to achieve at different stages in your journey, you will discover their evolving nature, and can use this information to help you change them in the future.

Go Long

Your story is not just about the past and present. You can add to your motivation and direction by extending your story into the future. You may decide, "I want to be a famous author," or "I want to earn my living as a writer," or "I want to use my writing as a tool for introspection and communication for the rest of my life." Give that dream more substance by consciously visualizing it.

At first the image may seem blurry. Take time to bring it into focus by allowing your imagination to drift forward to a time when you have already succeeded. From that vantage point, look back on the obstacles you overcame. Looking back on them takes away the mystery and fear, and makes them seem small.

WRITING PROMPT

> List some achievements that would make you feel good about your own writing. For example, imagine yourself in the future, after you have published the book you want to write. Someone has just thanked you for the difference your book has made in his life. In this future situation, look back at the process that brought you to this success. Free-write a story about what you did to achieve this goal. Focus on the things you have control over, like wit and effort, rather than things outside your control, such as lucky breaks.

YOUR ROLE AS A WRITER

When strangers meet, one often asks, "What do you do for a living?" You try to answer this simple question with a simple answer. *I'm a teacher, or a therapist. I'm in marketing, or computers. I'm a stay-at-home mom. I'm retired.* Based on this scrap of information, your listener draws conclusions about your background, effectiveness as a person, your role in society, and intentions for the future. That's a lot of information to pack into a single word or phrase.

When we label ourselves, or each other, we stir powerful emotions and images that link us to psychological states of mind. A simple label might sound depressing or joyful. In the *Think Like a Writer* section of this book, I show how labels help you manage your emotions. Labels also create social status. In this section, I focus on the way labeling yourself as a writer could help you identify yourself.

By calling yourself a writer, you declare your intentions, subtly shifting the emphasis from what you do for yourself to how you see your role in society. Like all role labels, this one comes with a host of implications. The obvious one is that you know how to put words together into a form that others will read. Your statement "I am a writer" carries with it the responsibility to open yourself up to the scrutiny and judgment of people you have never met. You are brave. You must bounce back from discouragement, face the possibility of rejection and sit for long hours, writing and revising.

Calling yourself a writer before you have published a bestseller might seem at first to be deceitful. "What if I sound like a pretentious liar? In that case, instead of admiration, I could earn scorn." But the fear of calling yourself a writer tends to wall you off from your goals.

When you say, "I'm a writer," you are not lying. You are stating the truth of your budding new role. When you call yourself a writer, you imagine yourself leaping over that wall, or breaking it down. Even when you are alone at your desk, you are reaching out to readers sometime in the future, somewhere in the world. You're not yet perfect nor will you ever be. Flaws in your work are normal parts of the writing process. You aspire to success, through a gradual increase in skills, material, and audience. By calling yourself a writer, you draw on some of the strength and wisdom of your fellow writers so you too can learn, grow, and succeed. All of these attributes accompany the label.

Your Evolving Contract with Society

When I was 18 years old, I was working in a medical school. My life unfolded before me like a book which had already been written. I was going to be a *doctor*.

But after several years in the state of confusion known as "The Sixties," I rejected all labels. *I am a person*, I thought, *and I have no need to define myself.* A person with no labels, however, lives in a vacuum. At first I attempted to fill that void by calling myself a *hippie*, implying a person who has no role in society. After a few years of this unstructured existence, I discovered that part time jobs couldn't satisfy my need for food, shelter, pride, or connection. It was too late to climb the mountain back to medical school, and so began my adult search for my new true role.

Thanks to my college degree in physics, I stumbled out of obscurity and landed a job in the nuclear power industry. The work satisfied my need for a paycheck, taught me how power plants generate electricity, and provided many interesting technical challenges. The new label, *engineer,* described my daily work, but when I said it out loud, it didn't seem to define *me*. A couple of years later, I switched to the computer industry. The label *programmer* seemed more chic. I switched again to write about computers and called myself a *technical writer*. When I received a master's degree in Counseling Psychology, I learned that the label *psychologist* is restricted by law to specific academic degrees. My training permitted me to call myself a *psychotherapist*. This label, like its predecessors, described only one of my roles. Fascinated by the years of experimentation and learning, I longed to pass my learning to others, a desire that opened me up toward the label, *writer*.

When I was younger, I used to think that a single label would lock me into one pigeonhole forever. Over the years, I realized labels change frequently. From one part of the day to the next, I considered myself a husband at home, a brother to my sister, and so on. From year to year, I wore a different label depending on my job. From decade to decade, I identified myself as a young man or an older one. This realization of the ever-changing nature of labels expanded my understanding of how to be a satisfied, well-rounded human being.

In *The Seven Habits of Highly Successful People*, Stephen Covey goes into detail about the importance of our many roles. He explains that our activities in one role, such as parent or spouse, can be just as important at home as our business activities are at the workplace. The concept of multiple simultaneous roles gave me permission to expand my passion for creative writing at home, while performing other services with equal vigor at the office.

If you think that "I am a writer" means you are only a writer, you reduce your ability to be a balanced, dynamic, multi-faceted person. By expanding your definition to permit multiple roles that shift and adapt as you grow, you improve your options to succeed in family, career, health, and creative expression.

WRITING PROMPT

> Write a short story about meeting someone new and introducing yourself with a more complete description than you can fit into one label. "Hi, I'm Mary, and even though I typically use one label to describe myself, I would love to tell you about this other aspect of myself."

WRITING IS A VAGUELY DEFINED ROLE

If you ask ten aspiring or accomplished writers, "Who ought to be allowed to call themselves writers?" you will probably hear ten different answers. In the most restrictive sense, you might recognize only those authors whose works are studied in high school or college literature classes. Another definition might be that a writer is someone who earns a living wage from the activity. Another might say the label ought to apply only to those who publish some number of books or articles, and still another might expect a writer to engage in that activity a minimum number of hours each day. In the broadest definition, everyone who has ever placed their thoughts, ideas, or stories into writing deserves the moniker.

Many careers involve writing. For example, people earn a living writing computer manuals, newspaper and magazine articles, grant applications, marketing literature, or speeches. Other people expect no compensation for writing poetry or submitting comments to newspapers. Freelancers attempt to make the leap from writing for themselves to writing for money. They hope to sell their articles, stories, novels, or poems. They could be published in commercial magazines, newsletters, e-zines, blogs, self- or traditionally published books, and so on.

Each of us decides at what point we will call any of these people "writers." And since the meaning of the term is so broadly defined, why not expand your definition to include yourself? By giving yourself permission to say "I am a writer" you can generate enthusiasm and confidence, using the label to help you grow toward your dreams.

LOFTY AND REMOTE

Throughout high school and college, my English teachers immersed me in the literary giants of our culture. We read and interpreted Chaucer, and Shakespeare, Proust and Joyce, whose works had influenced the course of literature itself. All the books in my courses stood the test of time, bearing up under close examination for generations. By my third reading of Charles Dickens' *Great Expectations*, I practically worshipped the author, whose turns of phrase and clever characters haunted my imagination. Mark Twain, Alexander Dumas, and many others lifted, informed, and entertained me. In response to their excellence, I elevated them to a plane of creative genius. When I began to write, I discovered that my zealous admiration for my favorite writers had a dark side. By raising them up to such lofty heights, I separated myself from their ranks. Since I would never qualify to join these demi-gods, why bother even trying?

CHILDHOOD IMPRESSIONS: INVISIBLE, PASSIVE, AND MAGICAL

Childhood images often establish our emotions for the rest of our lives. When I worked as a cashier at my father's drugstore, customers handed me money in exchange for goods. I greeted them, and performed the transaction courteously and competently. This highly visible role became part of my self-image.

As I neared the end of high school, I decided I would become doctor, a desire which captured my imagination so thoroughly I felt as if I was already a doctor and getting the degree was a mere detail. Those dreams of who I would become were influenced by what I saw. My father was a pharmacist, and we spoke reverently about physicians at home. Our family physician was a kind and important man. I wanted to be like him.

Children are exposed to all sorts of workers, in person and at home, and these images help us decide who we want to be when we grow up. We see postal workers, bus drivers, and teachers all doing their jobs. But few of us see writers engaged in the act of writing. If I occasionally saw a writer on the news, I gained no insight into his daily life.

Writers write in private. We send our work to editors we have never met, or we post it on the Internet, where people we can't see stop by to read. This distance makes it difficult for writers to see themselves in their readers' eyes.

By the time I graduated high school, despite having devoted myself slavishly to books, I had met no actual book writer. As a result, I saw books as magical gifts provided by invisible authors. I had no insight into how anyone might join their ranks.

WRITING PROMPT

Write a story about what non-writers think about writers. Do they look at writers as slackers and dreamers? Do they look at aspiring writers as desperate? Or do you think non-writers have admiration for the craft? Write a fictional account about a beginning or aspiring writer telling a stranger that he writes.

FEARS AND EMOTIONAL RESISTANCE TO "BEING A WRITER"

When you aspire to write, you might feel other anxieties lurking just under the surface. To move energetically toward your goal, consider any surreptitious concerns about seeing yourself in this role. For instance:

- If you are shy, you might be afraid that success will force you out of privacy and into uncomfortable public appearances.

- To sell your writing to an editor, a reader, or a bookstore, you must provide reasons why they should buy your work. This puts you in the unwelcome role of a salesperson.

- When you first began writing, you only had to please yourself–now you have a responsibility to please readers. You worry that writing for others will reduce the fun and turn it into a chore.

- You may not like people who call themselves writers, fearing that they are flaky, freewheeling, and unemployed.

Becoming more aware of your concerns gives you the opportunity to think each through in a more constructive way. Consider your goal, and weigh the benefits against your concerns. Pick off each of these mental objections so they can't undermine you.

WRITING PROMPT

Describe the aspects of becoming a writer that move you out of your comfort zone. After each such statement, answer back. For example, in response to "What if readers don't like me," respond "I'm happy to be known by readers. In fact, that's what this is all about." In answer to "I hate to convince anyone to read my writing," answer something like, "Of course I will need to help readers understand why they should read my work. Every piece of writing I've ever read has been presented to me through some sort of persuasion. Because I am offering them value, I will enjoy helping people find my writing." What other reasons discourage you from becoming a writer? After each reason for withdrawing from the challenge, offer a counterbalancing reason to press on.

Steps Toward Accepting "I am a Writer"

Once you accept the difficulties of calling yourself a writer, the next task is to overcome the obstacles and accept your new role. Here are some strategies you can use to move in that direction:

EXPAND YOUR DEFINITION TO INCLUDE SUB-SKILLS

Within the writer's role, we weave together a variety of activities, each with its own challenges and rewards. Consider this list of activities that may arise, fade, and change in the course of your writing project:

- Student - you learn new techniques
- Planner - you develop the outline of your project
- Writer ("I write") - you draft a passage that flows easily
- Explorer - you experiment with new material
- Editor - you review a piece to improve it
- Researcher or interviewer - you look for information
- Market researcher - you analyze your potential audience
- Goal seeker - you wonder, worry, and dream
- Author ("I publish") - you sell a piece or receive a glowing review
- Activist - you publicize an important message
- Inspirer - you encourage readers to reach for the next rung

Some of these tasks come more naturally to you than others. To succeed, however, all of the aspects of your job become important at some time or another. Your attitude toward each role could interfere with, or accelerate, your progress. For example, if you have the idea that writers are supposed to write perfect drafts the first time, you may resist editing and find yourself drowning in excellent but unpolished work. If you avoid marketing, you may develop wonderful material but never find readers. To achieve success, weave all these traits of the writer's life together to form a vibrant, colorful portrayal of your multi-faceted character.

WRITING PROMPT

> List the parts of yourself that influence you throughout your writing journey. Of the various roles you assume, which ones distract you from your goals? What parts of yourself propel you forward?

DO THE CRAFT

The more you write, the more the activity contributes to your sense of well-being. Writing can boost your self-confidence and creative satisfaction. By researching your pieces, you learn about the world and about yourself.

If you are unemployed, underemployed, or retired, engaging in this challenging activity helps maintain your sense of self-worth. Even if you are satisfied with your day job, spending your discretionary time in this creative pursuit can enrich your mind.

REACH READERS

Published pieces let you communicate with others and create a sense of community.

ASSOCIATE WITH OTHER WRITERS

Ostensibly, the reason for attending a group or class is to learn skills or to "network." In addition, these groups offer the important bonus of helping us see ourselves as writers among others like ourselves.

As you associate with other writers, enter workshops and competitions, and study books about writing, you earn your way deeper and deeper into the world of literary arts. Whether writing is your avocation or pursuit of a paycheck, by assuming the role of writer, you create connections between yourself and your entire culture.

A Metaphor Converts a Role-label into an Energetic Story

The physical act of writing does not necessarily provide an exciting picture. You sit at a desk, move your fingers, pause and stare, and then move your fingers more. These unimpressive visual scenes offer little to imagine when you try to describe your role. When you publish your work, however, you can inspire people, make them laugh out loud, or move them to tears, and you can offer them important ideas and information. To improve your energy, look beyond the prosaic image of a writer who sits at the desk, and step into the world of fantasy and metaphor. Metaphors engage the visual and story aspects of your mind, arousing archetypal characters and creatures. For example, in your role of writer you might think of yourself as a:

- Storyteller, bard, or minstrel
- Warrior against sloth and ignorance
- Teacher
- Star voyager or explorer
- All-seeing eagle, soaring above the land
- Angel, compassionate helper
- Unicorn, conveyor of spiritual light
- Sorcerer, alchemist, transforming the mundane with magic
- Mythological hero, overcoming hardship to serve the community

- Composer or musician

- Sculptor or architect

When students respond to this exercise in workshops, I am delighted by the metaphors they offer. For example, Judie visualized herself this way:

> "As a jester, I could choose to do a trick to fool the mind, or change and be funny, making the whole court laugh. I could pretend to be sad and bring pity and sorrow into the people's hearts, or I could be sly and sneaky, creeping around to scare a person. At the end of the day, I can remove my costume and just be me again, ready to resume my role at any given time or place."

I sometimes visualize myself as a farmer, tilling the soil, planting seeds, weeding, nurturing, reaping the harvest, and taking the fruits of my labor to market. I am fascinated by a farmer's list of responsibilities, such as repairing machinery, nurturing livestock, monitoring soil and water conditions, and managing finances. Even though few people actually see farmers at work, the product of their labor goes out to feed the rest of society. Tenacity and self-sacrifice are the hallmarks of farmers as well as writers.

WRITING PROMPT

Select your own metaphor. If one doesn't jump immediately to mind, relax, scan your imagination, and let yourself freely explore. Give your inner critic some time off. You're not looking for a "right" answer or a high score. When you have an image in mind, use your metaphor as the starting point to free-write a story about yourself in this role. In your story, would you speak at a podium, in a coffee shop, or at a campfire? How would you be dressed? Who would be in your audience? For example, "I am a wise owl coming out of hiding to reveal herself in the daylight" or, "As an alchemist, I will transform mundane reality into the gold of story that will change my life as well as the lives of others."

MAKE PEACE WITH OTHER CHARACTERS IN YOUR STORY

To fit writing into your discretionary time, you must take into account your relationship to the other characters in your life. Your parents, spouse, children, and others also play a part in this story. One way to "solve" the problem is to push people away. If family members feel rejected, however, they may escalate their demands and increase tension, hurting your relationships and your productivity. To maintain healthy writing habits as well as healthy relationships, develop conscious strategies to reassure people that you intend to fulfill your writing dreams, and at the same time, honor your social contracts.

In *The Seven Habits of Highly Effective People*, Stephen Covey recommends that instead of expecting relationships to take care of themselves, put some thought into building trust and mutual support with other people. By enhancing your contribution to family and community, you cultivate mutual respect. They recognize that you are doing your part, and are more likely to return the support. It may take time to take care of the people in your life, but in return, you gain the emotional support to carry on.

The emotional skill that helps you develop an effective, healthy balance with the people around you is called *assertiveness*. Assertiveness does not mean ignoring everyone else's needs. It just means you must take your own needs into account, and work toward balance. To become more assertive, first reaffirm your belief that you deserve to write. Second, effectively communicate your needs. We'll talk more about your beliefs later. For now, let's focus on communication.

Don't Expect Them to Read Your Mind

You will feel pushed around if other people communicate their needs more skillfully than you do. To meet them halfway, you need to clearly communicate the importance of your writing time. Many people, however, think it is wrong or rude to express their needs. Some people think, "If they loved and respected me, they would just know that I need to write." Expecting people to read minds is ineffective and creates tensions and resentment.

WRITING PROMPT

- Invent a scene and write the dialogue in which you tell a loved one that you need to write. What would you say? How would that person react? What would you say next?

- Write fictional scenes that exaggerate or extend your assertiveness training. Create a fictional character that tells various people how important it is to write. Use this character to help you get in touch with your own hopes and fears.

- Remember a time in your life when you asserted your needs and write that as a scene.

Negotiate: Use Your Words

Negotiating may sound business-like, but this technique offers many benefits in everyday life. Negotiating simply means spelling out what you want and what you're willing to give in return, and adjusting the give-and-take until both parties agree.

In each relationship where you are feeling pressure, develop a list of benefits that the other person will receive from your writing. Some possible negotiation points:

- You will set limits, and write during agreed-upon times.
- You will develop a system of rewards to let other people share in the achievement of your writing milestones.
- Give small gifts or unasked-for kindnesses, and let them know that joyful behavior results from their kindness to you during your writing time.

Go beyond mindreading by asking them to express their needs. Once their needs are out in the open, you can talk about them and move from a habit of silent assumptions to a healthy, communicative atmosphere.

One surprising bonus from these discussions might be the discovery that people in your life actually long for their own creative outlet. Instead of running away from their resentment, turn the tables and encourage them to pursue their own form of creative self-expression.

Once you learn the technique of negotiation, you can extend it to other areas of your life. Gradually, people around you will realize that it is OK to openly, explicitly discuss needs, and then maturely discuss the pros and cons of fulfilling them.

Your real-life learning will also improve your writing. By carefully observing the continuous balancing that takes place between your needs and the people around you, you will be able to improve the authenticity of characters in your stories and articles.

WRITING PROMPT

If some of your current approaches to people don't seem to be working, brainstorm to develop more effective methods. For example: With your family, agree upon schedules that give you time to write; move your writing to a more private space; get permission to turn off the phone for a specified period; budget money for babysitting or housecleaning. Write in your journal specific agreements you would like to make that would allow you more emotional space for your writing.

Wisdom Is More Productive than Blame

If you blame other members of your family or community for your own lack of productivity, you might be worrying too much about their influence and not enough about yours. For example, if you have to run an errand when you wish you could be writing, you might feel resentful and blame your lack of productivity on their demands. Such resentment wastes valuable energy. To succeed, focus as little energy as possible on blaming other people for your time constraints, and as much as possible on how to make the best use of whatever time you have available for yourself.

WRITING PROMPT

To bring your attention back to solutions that lie within your own reach, answer this question: "Instead of focusing on the role other people play, how can I improve my own actions and attitudes?"

Much of the pressure you may be attributing to the people around you may be emanating not from them but from inside yourself. For example resentment may arise from your guilt that you are not giving them enough, or fears they will stop loving you. You can develop a more trusting relationship with them by listening to them more carefully. Instead of fixating only on their negative emotions, take the whole mix into account. How would the conversation change if you assumed they love you and want you to be happy? By working toward their happiness and assuming they want yours, you turn a potential frustration into a win for everyone.

What Would Your First Teachers Think?

From the first words you uttered, your parents or other primary caregivers taught you what to say and how to say it. From those humble beginnings, your language skills continued to grow. Decades later, you wanted to become a writer, offering words to readers. To learn more about the emotions of communicating with strangers, imagine what your first language coaches might think.

WRITING PROMPT

Consider how you would feel if you were standing on a podium, beginning to read from your writing when you notice your parents in the audience. Would your voice become stronger and more confident or would you falter? Would you smile at them and make eye contact or avoid their gaze and try to pretend they weren't there?

After the talk, you greet them. Write a scene about such an encounter. Include an imagined discussion with them, and a description of your feelings. What would you expect them to say? Would they love your writing or hate it, be proud of you or wonder where you or they went wrong?

PUSHING FROM PRIVATE TO PUBLIC IS A FORM OF LAUNCHING

As we progressed through our teen years, we felt the call toward the next step in our lives. During that transition from child to adult, we learned how to interact with people outside the scope of our private lives. Some of us pushed away quickly, attempting to find our way in the world without looking back. Others lingered, living at home for extended periods or relying on parents for moral or financial support during the early stages of adulthood.

Becoming a writer requires you to launch again. To write for the public, you must shift your self-image from a private person to a public one. You must earn respect from people outside your circle, and figure out how to steer toward those who will support you. To prepare for this new launch, explore your previous ones to see if you can take advantage of your earlier lessons.

WRITING PROMPT

To learn more about the transition into your role as a writer, write a story about the period in your life when you evolved from teenager into adult. How supportive were your parents? Did your direction as an adult follow the lines they established? Or did you fling out into the world, without much concern about their response? How much did you have to fight with the world in order to be embraced by it?

During your struggle to break away the first time, you faced your anxiety and kept going. Eventually you learned how to participate in the larger world. Now that you want to become a writer, you might feel stirrings of that former anxiety. "Should I really do this?" "Can I handle the broader world on my own?" To face these challenges, get back in touch with your former courage. As a young adult, you acquired self-awareness, and expertise. By writing about that transition, you will intensify your relationship to it, providing insights that can help you face this new one.

Another aspect of your teenage years that could ease your transition into life as a writer is your relationship to peers. Back then, these relationships played an important role.

Banding together with others in your situation helped you gain courage. Consider applying a similar powerful tool of companionship to help you become a writer.

When I went to college in the 1960s, I leaned on my peers to help me revise my self-definition. In cliques and parties, we experimented, encouraged one another, and commiserated about the difficulties of progressing to the next step. My transition was marred, however, because during those years of anti-war riots, millions of men and women in battle, drugs and the counter-culture, my peers were as confused as I was. My reliance on their guidance created more missteps and longer recoveries than if I had sought help from those who had already succeeded.

As an adult writer, I again turned to my peers. Writing groups and classes provided a forum to support and exhort each other. These cliques and cadres remind me of the best aspects of being a teen. In both eras, we redefine ourselves with the companionship and support of others who are trying to do the same. Fortunately, my adult peers are far more mature and knowledgeable than my teenage friends were. In the writing community, there is an ample supply of helpful advice from those who have achieved success.

WRITING PROMPT

Imagine yourself attempting to overcome some barrier in your writing life. Say you are attempting to finish a piece, or trying to build up the nerve to submit it to a publication. Instead of picturing yourself as a lonely voice in the wilderness, write a scene where you are out with your teenage friends. Choose your characters for this imagined vignette in one of two ways. Use your actual teen friends, but pretend they are all writers, trying to find agents. Or . . . use your current writing pals, but pretend they are teenagers, hanging out at the local diner, or doing whatever teenagers do to assert their right to be themselves.

In your vignette, listen to courageous stories about how your friends are sending out queries. Use the shared courage of those images to create a more focused, intense image of your own mission.

GIVE PARENTS PERMISSION TO GROW UP

Even when we're fully grown adults, our parents sometimes remind us we were once tiny children. During an argument or power struggle, these reminders evoke emotions of helplessness and vulnerability. If being around your parents or even thinking about them evokes feelings of being out of control, naturally you attempt to distance yourself from them or their reactions. There is, however, a psychological cost for prying yourself loose from your parents and other primary caregivers. Because they are so much a part of you, ripping them out of your life can tear you apart. Instead of fighting to keep them away, consider other ways to include them in your process.

One method is to simply acknowledge their position, whatever it is. Lament it, or even respect it, as being normal for people with their background. In other words, accept it as their truth even though it is not your own. By not fighting with your parents' perspective, you will reduce the effort of worry and judgment, and you won't need to work so hard to keep them away.

Another way to approach this challenge is to view your relationship as a story that evolves over time. By looking for the change across decades, you may be able to create a more dynamic way of experiencing their roles in your life as a writer.

For many years, I was sure that my parents would never be able to understand me as an adult. When my mother was in her 80s, I finally attempted to break through this barrier. I talked to her weekly, avoiding our hot buttons and persistently pursuing topics that genuinely interested both of us. In addition to the usual news about the extended family, I was delighted to discover we both loved to talk about books. The experiment worked and revealed an interesting new dimension of our relationship.

I realized that until then, I had been doing the same thing to my mother as I feared she was doing to me. I was locking her into the old patterns we had established decades earlier. When I took a closer look, however, I discovered that over the course of time, my mother had been growing, too.

There is an old truism in child-rearing: "Children don't need you to be their friends. They need you to be their parents." But as I grew older, this logic reversed. Later in life, I no longer wanted my parents to tell me what to do. I wanted them to be my friends. By challenging myself to see my mother as a peer, I allowed my image of her to "grow up."

If you don't have the opportunity to revisit your relationship in real life, you may be able to achieve similar results in fantasy. This is a variation on the familiar exercise of "silencing the inner critic." Instead of focusing on your inner critic, develop a knack for inviting inner supporters.

One day, while wishing I could feel support from both my parents, I looked up from my computer and imagined them "listening" to my writing. They leaned forward in their chairs, smiling when I wrote something comical. And when I crafted an interesting point, they nodded thoughtfully as if they were taking it all in.

My parents, in real life, are no longer alive, so the event took place only in my imagination. And yet, despite its lack of physical reality, their presence warmed me. By befriending them in my imagination, they became part of my supportive audience, my "inner circle fans." And by imagining them in this way, I give them the gifts of trust and respect that I have always wanted to receive from them.

One of the most hopeful elements in a good story is the way characters evolve over time. By crafting your parents as evolving characters in your story, you can feel this uplifting element in your own journey to become a writer.

Chapters in Our Lives

An ill parent, a newborn baby, or a new career may intrude so forcefully into your schedule that you can't find a single moment to devote to your writing. Even then, you still have the freedom of imagination. Hang on to that freedom. Instead of letting your thoughts drag you into a sense of helplessness, maintain a playful, hopeful view of your unfolding journey. Imagine yourself as a character in the long story of your life. Your desire burns under the surface. Interruptions are simply detours on the road toward success.

TRAVEL THE HERO'S JOURNEY TO WRITING SUCCESS

Suppose you are watching a movie in which the hero must rescue his lover from an enemy stronghold. He climbs a mountain and approaches an armed outpost that stands between him and his goal. Realizing that the mission is dangerous, he suddenly remembers that he has a dentist appointment that afternoon, and so he turns around and goes home. Cut! That's not the way stories work.

We expect our heroes to persist, to learn from mistakes, and to overcome obstacles. Above all, we expect heroes to keep moving forward, even if they encounter discomfort or danger. Our vicarious thrill of experimentation and risk draws us forward in our seats.

Mythologist Joseph Campbell studied the characteristics of folk heroes passed down through millennia. His lifetime of study revealed fascinating parallels among military heroes, spiritual leaders, folk legends, and mythical gods. Apparently, the ancient themes of the hero's journey have riveted our attention since across a vast variety of cultures throughout history. Nowadays, movie writers study Campbell's ideas to ensure their stories satisfy our passion for heroes. Heroic action is so universal it seems to be built into our collective consciousness, our genes, our very souls.

For an in-depth account of Campbell's system of myth, read his classic work, *A Hero with a Thousand Faces*. To learn how to apply the system to fiction writing, read the far-more-accessible guide by Christopher Vogler, *The Writer's Journey*. Once you understand the concepts, you can apply them to your own experiences by characterizing yourself as the hero of your own writing journey. Use this ancient tool to help you focus so intently on your goals that your discomfort fades into the background, a mere inconvenience to brush aside as you strive confidently onward. One thing heroes can't tolerate is stagnation. Don't let any more time slip by without pressing onward.

To help you cast yourself in this role, I've summarized the stages described by Joseph Campbell and Chris Vogler.

The Familiar World

At the beginning of the classic hero story, we meet the central character living in a familiar world. For example, at the beginning of *Star Wars*, Luke Skywalker focuses on chores he must perform around the farm. In *The Wizard of Oz*, Dorothy also talks to farmhands. Their mundane worries establish our identification with an ordinary person who faces challenges similar to our own.

The reader then wants the story to become more intense, so part of the job of this introduction is to reveal the seeds of discontent. What in this "normal" world is out of balance and needs to change? Perhaps the character has a secret desire, or something is not quite as it seems, or perhaps there are forces at work to make the ordinary world dangerous. In *Star Wars*, Luke Skywalker has a secret past, and his family is living under the cloud of that past. In *The Wizard of Oz*, Dorothy fears that there is no place for a dreamer like her.

Before becoming a writer, ordinary responsibilities dominate our days and "becoming a writer" seems far away, perhaps even impossible. Like Dorothy's belief that her dreams lie "somewhere over the rainbow," we assume that satisfaction for this creative impulse lies in the distant future.

We fear we don't have enough time or training or connections. We can't imagine that strangers would ever read our work, or we fear that only arrogant dreamers would expect anyone to read what they had written. We may hide our writing, feeling too shy to show it even to intimate friends.

WRITING PROMPT

> Many writers remember moments when they wrote in secret, hid a diary, or felt mortified when their writing was discovered. Write a scene when you felt your writing was private, and would never be known by anyone in the world.

The Hero is Called or Booted into Action

The action of the story begins when the problem becomes so compelling that the protagonist can no longer remain in the ordinary world. The "call to go forth" arrives in various forms. Sometimes a threat forces the hero to face a new challenge. Luke Skywalker receives a mysterious message from a damsel in distress, asking him to leave his familiar world and enter a new one. When he finds that his home has been destroyed, he is forced to enter the adventure. In *The Wizard of Oz*, Dorothy believes that to protect her dog, she must run away.

The pressures that force us to write are complex. Writers feel pressured to write because they are good at it, because they love the feeling of it, or because it seems to be a way to earn a living that only requires the raw material inside their own minds. Some write because it is a great hobby, or because they admire the people who create stories, articles, and books and they want to do the same for others. Some write because of a creative urge or because they want to teach, or leave a legacy.

So when you look for the cause that forced you into this heroic journey, you might feel somewhat bewildered by the stew of reasons. If you can't think of a particular motivating force, you may need to resort to metaphor or mysticism, considering your calling to the writing life as a mission, a destiny, an inner knowing, or a search for Truth.

WRITING PROMPT

> What is driving you to write? It may be a vague desire for creative self-expression or it may be a vivid image of exactly what you must accomplish. How would you express your Call: practical ("I want to earn a living as an author"), psychological ("It will help me feel good about myself"), metaphorical ("I want to touch the stars"), or metaphysical ("The pleasure of writing lifts my soul.")? Write a scene or anecdote about the pressure that pushed you to become a writer.

Reluctant Hero: Refusing or Denying the Call

When the Call first arrives, the hero faces a choice: remain in the comforts of home or enter the danger of the unknown. When Luke is first summoned to help Princess Leia, he demurs, complaining that his family needs him on the farm. In *The Wizard of Oz*, when Dorothy first runs away, she encounters a circus wizard who convinces her to return home.

When you consider becoming a writer, you are drawn by creative incentive. But you also may be conscious of the price you'll pay. You may fear that writing for an audience will wreck the spontaneity and pleasure of your work. You may fear you won't have enough time or energy. Are you willing to risk disapproval? Is this what you really want?

By exploring the spectrum of your feelings, you can expose lurking misgivings and find the courage to proceed anyway. Don't turn back now. Adventure awaits!

WRITING PROMPT

> In your journal, imagine a debate between two parts of yourself, one who wants to face the challenges and become a writer and one who prefers privacy and relaxation. Include intense, even exaggerated reasoning. Allow the debate to range far into possible disasters and possible successes. Explore the range of feelings that hold you back, and the range of possibilities that await your discovery.

Cross into the World of the Adventure

The pressure grows, and finally the hero "crosses the threshold," moving from the familiar world into the land of the adventure. In *Star Wars*, when Luke Skywalker embarks on his adventure, he visits the cantina, where all sorts of peculiar creatures relax and enjoy each other's company. Luke looks around, stunned that these weird creatures think he's the odd one. Similarly, Dorothy leaves a drab farmhouse, where farmhands feed pigs, and enters a colorful land where munchkins dance, monkeys fly, and tin men talk.

I have met many writers for whom the first inkling they could become writers came during a particular workshop or writing conference. Perhaps for you it was while reading a book, or speaking to a mentor. Or perhaps this was a dream that had been nagging you for years, and at some point, something prompted you to stop dreaming about it and start acting.

WRITING PROMPT

> What changes in your inner or outer world signaled your commitment to the writing life? Did you begin to experiment with writing styles, take classes, attend poetry readings, study books about the craft, join a group, or submit a story? If you are not sure, pick any event in your journey, or imagine one in your future and free-write about how it affects your rules and goals.

As a writer, instead of using discretionary time for relaxing, you feel compelled to work on a piece, or attend a writing group. Writing competes with familiar roles and draws us into new territory, where we strive to please strangers and transform images into words. Writing is humbling. The journey is so long, with so many new beginnings. In a sense, every new sentence is a new beginning.

Becoming a writer is an exciting transition. We learn and apply the rules, hang out with people of similar intent, develop writing habits, and in general, become acclimated to the world of the adventure.

Obstacles Make the Story Go and the Hero Grow

On every great journey, heroes encounter obstacles. Some obstacles might be external: not enough money or time; lack of support or too much responsibility; a world that seems indifferent to our message. Some obstacles are based on the past, such as the lack of coursework in creative writing. Other obstacles are psychological: We must overcome fears, cope with frustration, and break through misconceptions about ourselves.

If you feel derailed by the things that interfere with your goals, take a lesson from heroes. To reach the goal, they must have at least as much respect for their own competence as they have for the things that try to block them. Heroes approach obstacles, cope with the fear, decide on a strategy, and then charge ahead.

As you conquer each challenge, you grow. Before long, you look back and realize that scary challenges no longer threaten you. Instead of interfering with your goals, these challenges now appear in the rear-view mirror as events that fostered your development. Your own trials and achievements enhance your writing as well as your appreciation for the variety and scope of human experience.

There's no need for regret. You could even honor these past obstacles. Build a shrine by the side of the road to commemorate the victory of overcoming each one.

> "[Some writers] . . . find excuses for not writing at the same time every day, balk at re- revising incessantly, or excuse themselves because their lives are beset by difficulties. I am deaf to that excuse because I worked with the most disadvantaged writer in history. Christy Brown, who had the use of his brain, the little toe on his left foot, and little else. When he was a seemingly helpless baby lying on the kitchen floor of a cottage in Ireland, his remarkable mother saw him reach out with his left foot and with his good toe manage to pick up a crayon that one of his siblings dropped. . . . I published five of Christy Brown's books, one of which made the national bestseller lists."
> From *Stein on Writing* by Sol Stein.

WRITING PROMPT

Think back over your history as a writer, and imagine yourself a few years ago. Perhaps you had not yet started your training, or had never finished a structured piece, or had to wake up in the middle of the night to care for someone who needed you. Write a paragraph about your feeling of helplessness and frustration, seeing your writing goals off in the distance, with so many problems interfering with your ability to ever reach them. Then, write a story about how your optimism, determination, and tenacity kept you going.

Now consider current obstacles. Use imagination and optimism to describe how these circumstances are catalysts that will help you grow to the next step. These setbacks will even provide material for your future writing. Your success gives you depth and even expertise at facing and overcoming such problems, perhaps enabling you to help others cope with similar challenges.

Team with Your Band of Allies

Most of us associate the word "hero" with self-reliance. But when you consider heroic stories, in almost every case, the heroes' allies contribute to the heroes' success. In Homer's *Odyssey*, when Ulysses' shipmates died, he turned to the gods for help. When he returned home, he teamed up with his own son, Telemachus. In *Star Wars*, Luke Skywalker depended on the advice of mentors, the assistance of sidekicks, and the support of literally an army of helpers. In *The Wizard of Oz*, Dorothy leaned on the Good Witch,

Lion, Scarecrow, and Tin Man. And in *The Lord of the Rings*, Frodo relied on the Fellowship.

As writers, we too, make progress on our journeys by aligning ourselves with allies. We join groups, attend conferences, and participate in programs where fellow writers offer mutual support and feedback. They provide a creative safety net, add a social element to an otherwise isolated activity, and make our goals feel more attainable. By sharing the stage with these energizing allies, we bolster our self-image as writers.

Some potential allies need to be recruited. When you first pitch your work to an agent or editor, you might fear they will never help. As you gain experience, you gradually learn how to work with them. Together you can accomplish more than you could alone.

WRITING PROMPT

List and describe people who have given you a boost on your journey. Write scenes to show the depth they have added to your writing journey. Brainstorm how you can enlist more allies or draw greater support from the ones you already have.

Acquire Skills and Knowledge Along the Way

When heroes enter the adventure, they must learn new skills. To do so, they rely on teachers as well as on the lessons they learn through experience. In *Star Wars*, Obi Wan Kenobi shows Luke how to use the lightsaber. He tells Luke that to work the unfamiliar weapon he must "feel the Force." One reason the scene resonates so profoundly with audiences is the implication that the power of a lightsaber emanates from the strength and goodness of the person who wields it. The same may be said of the power of the pen.

Courage is one of the most important lessons a hero must learn, and it is acquired as a result of facing fear. As Dorothy in *The Wizard of Oz* attempts to find the path home, she learns to fight for her own rights and to protect her friends. By confronting the evil witch and the dishonest wizard, she grows strong.

Aspiring writers also grow strong. We accept our need to improve language skills, so we read books and attend workshops. We face the pressures of distraction and we learn to push through anyway. We cope with the fear that readers might not like us, yet we keep reaching out to them.

In peer critique groups, feedback allows us to consider our writing through others' eyes. Critique groups also teach us how to edit. Working together in the group, we come to understand writing as a social act, in which mutual support plays a crucial role.

When exploring the story of our journey to become writers, we discover skills hiding in surprising places. One woman in my workshop complained that she felt so much pressure to excel at her writing that it was no longer a joyful activity. Then her face lit up when she remembered the innocent pleasure of teaching her son how to turn his verbal stories into written ones. She decided that by mentoring young people, she could improve her self-confidence and momentum.

As hero-writers we gain an appreciation for the power of time. We grow through years of striving. Patience and persistence are important allies throughout the long journey to success.

WRITING PROMPT

In previous writing prompts, you gathered a list of moments when writing was important to you. For this writing prompt, look at the list as if it represented a writing class, not that you took in a school, but that was embedded in the journey of your life. Now describe the way those lessons added up as if you were describing a multi-year program of study.

Include insights into the craft of putting sentences together or structuring pieces. For example, remember lessons about writing dialogue, or structuring stories. Also include small victories, such as when you figured out how to sneak more writing time into your schedule by waking up early.

If you remember the exact moment when one of these realizations occurred, write the scene, reproducing the situation as if you were there. Extend your scene into a story, developing your self-image as an aspiring writer who lacked this information, and then went to the right place to find it.

This written description of your writing lessons, sorted into chronological order, forms a resumé or diary of your development as a writer. Keep adding to it as you gain new insights.

For example, here are a few of my favorite aha moments:

1995
From a dog-eared paperback my wife's father gave me, I learned how to line up sentences so the end of one feeds into the beginning of the next.

1998
From *Language Instinct* by Steven Pinker, I learned that ambiguous sentences force the reader to backtrack. When revising, always try to weed out such unintended ambiguity.

1999

In an online course, writing-mentor Joseph O'Connor said, "If you want to write, don't set vague goals. You need specific projects." I decided to write articles about self help. From the project, I developed a website, a writing habit, and a self-image as a writer.

2000

I had never written a story and assumed I never would. On a weeklong retreat, I read Robert McKee's book called *Story* and by the end of that week realized that story writing is a learnable skill.

2002

I always thought writing was a solo activity. In 2002, I joined a store-front writing club called the Writers Room, where writers gathered for workshops and critique groups. By joining this community and seeing myself as "one of this group" I learned that becoming a writer connected me with other writers, and gave me a new insight into the role of a writer.

2004

Writing mentor Jonathan Maberry said, "Your writing isn't personal enough. It feels like it is falling from the sky. Put more of yourself into it." I took his suggestion to heart, attended a memoir workshop and began to learn the value of finding my own story in order to share myself with others.

2004

In a memoir writing class, mentor Foster Winans said "Learn about your past by interviewing other people. Ask them what they thought of you." Foster's advice showed me how memoir authors live both on and off the page. I learned techniques for character development, and also advanced my understanding of using story-of-self as a self help technique.

2005

I was terrified of public speaking, so I joined Toastmasters International. When I gave my first speech, I saw my audience laugh, yawn, or stare politely. From then on, when I crafted each speech, I imagined my audience's reaction. I incorporated this realization into my writing sessions, challenging myself to anticipate the response from readers.

2006

In a critique group, someone said, "I counted the word 'get' ten times in this piece." I looked at his editing marks. Each use of the word was reasonable, but together, they sounded ridiculous. Before that session, I might have revised the piece many times without noticing repetition. After that session, I became much more conscious of the insidious tendency to repeat words.

2011

In a workshop, author-turned-agent Marie Lamba said, "A good story has at least two ticking clocks." Her suggestion for building tension through the pressure of time fascinated me for two reasons. One was the technique itself. I could revise my own work or critique others based on the effectiveness of their ticking clocks. The second reason for my fascination was that the life of a story writer has a ticking clock. We try to improve, and each year, we gather aha moments, insights, and techniques that contribute to our climb toward excellence.

The Long Middle Provides Time to Grow

When the hero first begins the journey, readers share the excitement of a new adventure. But over time, hero and reader settle into the drudgery of the "long middle." During the middle, the tension to reach the goal is covered over with fatigue. Discouragement rears its head. Moses spent 40 years trying to reach Israel. Ulysses traveled for many years attempting to return to his home in Ithaca. In modern epics like *The Lord of the Rings,* a band of heroes marches through and over mountains to reach the foreign lands of the enemy.

Despite the apparent drudgery, the long middle serves an important function. Audiences know that authentic change doesn't happen overnight. The long middle gives the character time to grow and change.

Your epic journey to become a writer will also take time. You can't reach the top of a creative mountain in the first week, or even the first year. Successful writing takes longer than you expect. At times, goals seem distant and hopelessly unattainable.

Your long-term success requires grace, strength, and tenacity. Set modest goals, and feel satisfied by small victories, knowing they add up over time. Overcome impatience, ignore discomfort, and maintain focus on the mission. Band together with allies, seek help from mentors, learn skills, and above all, maintain the courage and determination of hero-writers throughout history who kept going despite the length of the journey.

During this period, as you overcome obstacles and develop skills, you gradually incorporate writing into your self-image. Even your brain takes time to adapt, as your neurons grow and rewire to so you can turn writing into a meaningful component of your life.

During the long middle, you need supportive relationships with spouse, children, parents, and friends. At times, their needs seem to distract you. And yet, these are the people who make the journey worthwhile. Instead of trying to work around them, enlist them as allies, and support their own long journeys to inner satisfaction.

Occasionally, during a Hero's Journey, instead of worrying about the pressure of tomorrow, take a moment to look back. Compared with a few years ago, you're making progress, learning and achieving more than you thought possible. Climbing this mountain is difficult, but through persistence, you make progress.

In fiction, the protagonist's ferocious efforts are often fueled by a commitment to serve a lover. Writers can tap into that raw power by thinking of readers as lovers. We woo them. We long for their admiration and return the favor by admiring them. We serve them with words. We please them, inform them, and share with them.

WRITING PROMPT

> Describe methods that have helped you overcome dead spots in your energy (e.g., took a class, hired a coach, read a self-help book).
>
> Become your own helpful advisor and write a motivational speech, explaining to yourself how to maintain enthusiasm through the middle of the journey.

Stymied at the Gates of the Inner Sanctum

When the hero reaches the end of the long middle, the journey is not finished. The prize lay ahead, surrounded by walls, hundreds of feet high. The fortress is so heavily guarded, it is difficult to imagine ever entering.

In *Star Wars*, when Luke Skywalker attempts to rescue the princess, he must invade the Death Star, bypassing computerized defense systems and legions of battled-hardened soldiers. In the *Odyssey*, when Ulysses finally reaches home, he finds his wife surrounded by ruthless men. He must fight against impossible odds. Instead of entering the city as an enemy, he disguises himself and dresses as a harmless old beggar. The legions of men allow him to enter freely. In *The Wizard of Oz*, when Dorothy's friends want to enter the witch's fortress, they obviously can't succeed by using force. Instead they disguise themselves as insiders and enter unchallenged. Brilliant.

As a writer, after struggling to learn skills and develop pieces that you believe are worthy of publication, you reach the gates of the publishing world and must somehow be granted admission. You tirelessly attempt to enter by editing and revising, searching for agents, or learning the steps of self-publishing. After each surge, you feel a little more deserving, but you are not inside yet.

You wish someone from inside the fortress would come outside to say, "I've heard you were out here. Please come in." But so far no one has done that. Instead, you become a beggar at the fortress gates, and watch as insiders come and go. You must figure out how to maintain momentum, despite this seemingly insurmountable blockade.

Then you realize you have been preparing for this final challenge all along. Throughout the long middle, you have been adjusting yourself to the role of the writer.

Through struggles to complete pieces, find outlets for your writing, and intrigue readers, you have learned how to look, sound, act, and even think like a writer.

In workshops, conferences, and groups, you hobnob with others who are also trying to become writers, as well as those who have already succeeded. You grow more knowledgeable about what is required to be an insider. You steel your courage, develop strategies, and keep trying. You look for the wellspring of strength within yourself: in faith, in hope, in the need to fulfill your mission, in the desire that drove you this far, and in the soulful longing for something that transcends your "ordinary world."

Within reach of your goal, so close you feel like you could reach out and touch it, you search for any small step that would increase your chances of entering. Here are a couple of practical ways to "penetrate the fortress" and mingle with the "insiders" before you actually become "one of them:"

- Volunteer at a writing club. Writers will thank you for helping to bring them together. When you organize events, you can invite writers, editors, and agents to come and speak, creating a personal relationship with individuals who are "inside the fortress."

- Start a blog in which you review books. As the blog grows, you will be able to ask increasingly influential authors for interviews, gaining an insider perspective to their thoughts and ideas.

- Take a course from an agent. For a modest fee, I attended an all-day writing class with agent Sheree Bykofsky. On a different occasion, I took a course from agent Marie Lamba. Spending hours in their company, I was introduced to two kind, smart women who were willing to share the secrets of the agenting business. These small investments helped me turn agents from scary gatekeepers into potential allies and friends.

WRITING PROMPT

During your journey to reach the gates, you have already demonstrated tenacity and passion. To bolster your courage, list the steps you have already taken to reach this point.

Write about times when you tried to cross thresholds into writing. For example, you reached out to publishers, or joined a writing group. Describe your experiences. How does it feel to receive acceptance and praise? How about criticism and rejection? Honor each such crossing or attempted crossing as part of your heroic development as a writer.

Develop a strategy to pass the gates. For example, submit your pieces to readers and gatekeepers. What sorts of additional preparations would be useful? As if you were an advisor, write a letter to yourself, coaching how to improve the areas of preparation that will be needed for success.

WRITING PROMPT

Instead of worrying about your next obstacle, look back on past achievements. Write a story about a situation in which you overcame obstacles and entered a new world, such as a new school, relationship, career, country, and then over time, mastered that situation.

WRITING PROMPT

Instead of feeling stressed about how to cross an intimidating threshold, use your imagination to leap into the future and look back. Write a story in which you imagine you have already succeeded in your writing goal. For example, imagine you have already published your book. Then creatively construct a story about all the obstacles that blocked you and the victories that brought you to this point. In addition to confidence, this exercise might give you some good ideas about how to proceed.

The Hero Dances with Death

In *The Lord of the Rings*, when Frodo first ventures out of the protective shell of his cozy village, he crosses the threshold into a more vulnerable world, where he is attacked by assassins, magic forces, and entire armies. Despite these dangers, he presses on.

The threat of death plays a key role in stories, first leading the hero to the brink of oblivion and then awakening surprising reservoirs of strength. When courage arises from the depths of despair, readers and viewers are filled with hope. We think, *Perhaps, in adversity, I too, could summon that level of integrity and vigor.*

As writers, we regularly face the death of our creative dreams. The demands of work and family and the difficulty of reaching audiences sometimes make success seem out of reach. *What if I can never achieve a worthwhile goal? Will I ever fulfill these inner longings? Is this a waste of time?* Setbacks pierce us to the core, and if we look directly into the darkness, all hope is lost.

Instead of yielding to discouragement, view your failures as steps along your heroic journey. In fact, a story without obstacles would barely be a story at all. The greater the challenge, the more satisfying the triumph. When you have a sense of purpose, your goals always return, drawing you relentlessly. Like all heroes, in the moment of despair, writers remember the quest, and return to it again and again.

Viktor Frankl was one such writer. After working for years with patients who threatened suicide, he realized that having a sense of purpose makes the difference between mental health and mental despair. To spread the urgent importance of maintaining a goal, he wrote a manuscript for a book on that subject. When the Nazis shipped him to a death camp in the 1940s, their first act of violence against him was to confiscate the manuscript. That was only the beginning of unspeakable humiliation, followed by torture. If anyone had the right to give up on life, he did. The assaults on Frankl's personhood are the stuff of fantastical battles between good and evil. And like the hero of such a story, he clung to his dreams by a thread.

After Frankl staggered to freedom at the end of the war, he rewrote his book and went on to become a world-renowned proponent of the importance of finding meaning. His intimate familiarity with death helped shape the wisdom he shared with millions.

Even far less dire setbacks might raise the possibility that momentum is lost and success out of reach forever. If we cling to the belief that the game is over, we will, like Frankl's fellow prisoners in the death camp, give up and die. If instead we look at valleys as horrible but necessary stages along a heroic journey, we will return to the challenge.

Defeat empties us so that we can be scrubbed out and refilled, ready for new and more exciting triumphs. Spring reveals the purpose of winter, and rebirth reveals the purpose of death. We shed layers of self-defense and become more vulnerable to our readers who feel a kinship with our authentic dreams and want more.

You can even recover from smaller deaths by allowing them to renew your courage. Turn hassles and distractions into the psychological tension of a good story. What would a hero do when facing discomfort, rejection, and even the fear of death? Instead of seeing each defeat as final, think of it as a step along the path, an obstacle that will force you to grow and learn. By the end of your long journey, you will look back on the difficulties and realize they contributed to your authentic success.

WRITING PROMPT

> Write about an incident when you revived your enthusiasm after a creative slump. Write about how it felt to face and overcome the loss of momentum. If you are currently experiencing a dip in your writing desires, describe what that loss feels like. Free-write about how you will get started again. In your story, envision this period as a rest stop on the road to success.
>
> Or accentuate the power of this setback, and script your downturn as a symbolic "death" – perhaps the death of your pride or

ambition. Allow your imagination to be drawn relentlessly toward the resurrection that will follow.

To awaken hope for the future, write about a situation when you will experience satisfaction after reaching your next milestone.

The Hero Brings Wisdom Back to the Community

When heroes leave home at the beginning of a story, they are getting away from mundane life and going on an adventure. When they complete that adventure, the natural resting spot is often back home.

After the adventure, the hero accepts a new role. He or she brings back important knowledge from the land of the adventure. The hero's knowledge of what lies beyond the boundaries of the kingdom become the legends of the community.

At the end of *Star Wars*, Luke walks down the aisle amid cheers from the throngs of well wishers. In a cozier hero story, when Dorothy returns from Oz, her family is joyously happy to see her. In Native American myths, heroes often bring magic, wisdom, and knowledge to their community. Their courage to undergo the adventure benefits everyone.

In traditional societies, elders are respected for the experience they have gained from their long journeys. In modernity, respect for elders has waned, but there is one kind of wisdom we continue to celebrate. When writers provide stories, the wisdom contained within them flows to readers. And readers respond with money, praise, and a thirst for more.

When the hero first sets out on the adventure, it looks like a lonely journey, with no discernible relationship to the public. By the end, though, the returned adventurer has become a respected messenger. Those who reach the end of the journey are no longer living just for themselves. They become public figures and what they say–and how they say it–matters.

To move into the public eye, writers must venture beyond the protected self-image of a private person to the unbounded scope of a public one. We leave behind the good old days when we were sitting, unknown, at our computers. Now our success depends on the reactions of strangers.

In the *Love Like a Writer* section of this book, I talk more about the complexities and importance of moving from private to public life.

WRITING PROMPT

What does your writing offer to your family, community, or the world? What expression of appreciation do they offer in exchange? How does your role as a writer change your relationship to your community?

How will success change your life? For example, would you be comfortable having your picture featured in the news? Do you have fantasies of winning awards and recognition? Do these fantasies attract, frighten, or confuse you? For most of us, success will be modest, with a mix of published writing and other roles. Write about this intertwining of public and private life, checking to see if it is harmonious with your image of who you are, and what you want.

Write Your Own Hero's Journey

To become a writer, apply the powerful metaphor of the Hero's Journey to your life. By inserting your own experience into this structure, you will see yourself in a new way. Ordinary life, when interpreted through the powerful metaphor of the Hero's Journey, lends itself to heroic self-sacrifice and tenacious determination.

In addition, writing your life story provides a fabulous learning opportunity. Like a Renaissance artist using a self-portrait to increase the sensitivity to nuances of character, your attempts to write a life story will increase your wisdom about the inner lives of characters and the structure of stories.

To start the exercise, gather facts about your writing life as if you were writing a memoir. For example, write about the time a sibling read your diary and you felt violated. Or write about the first time you read a story that felt so real and strong you were sure it changed your life. Or draft a story about a time when you wrote your first poem or article. From these snippets, write scenes that show the reader how you felt, what you wanted, and what you saw.

Such scenes, when first crafted, provide raw material for your story but they lack cohesion. Connect facts and anecdotes into a coherent whole by weaving them into the Hero's Journey. Write about your ordinary world with its built-in tensions. Write about receiving the Call, and crossing the threshold into the world of the adventure. Show how allies bolstered your courage, and new skills enhanced your progress. If you have not yet approached the fortress, imagine yourself doing so. Write a story about how you plan to pass through those gates. Project even farther, and imagine how, once you have passed through those gates, you will accept your new role. Then, to complete your journey, you will return to offer your hard-earned wisdom to your community. Imaginatively match the events of your writing life with the stages of the journey. Have fun as you creatively visualize your role as the hero in your own story.

Seeing your life through this metaphor can help at every stage. You can trade self-doubt for courage. You can reach out toward allies and training when you feel stuck. You can draw strength during the long middle. And by seeing yourself as a character in a story, you can link the disparate parts into a creative whole.

Visualizing your life as a Hero's Journey helps you convert old regrets into stages along the path. And you can apply the metaphor to your new challenges, continually relying on heroic tenacity, courage, and wisdom. Where you are exactly in the journey is subject to interpretation. Even after you have made it to the inner sanctum and then returned, you may discover you have another journey you must take to a new challenge, or a new stage in your creative life.

By starting with the stages as described here, or by reading Chris Vogler's *Hero's Journey*, or by attempting to emulate the elements of your favorite hero stories, you can turn and bend the events of your writing life into a courageous, inspiring story that will help motivate and energize you. Heroes rely on the confidence that victory is inevitable, and as the hero of your own journey, so can you.

The most rewarding revelation of the Hero's Journey for me was recognizing the pervasive notion of "giving back." Once I realized its importance, I began to see it everywhere. The hero of the story, as well as the writer of that story, contributes to the wisdom of his audience.

When the hero returns from the adventure, the community gathers around to listen. They want to know "what lies in the world you visited." On the surface, their interest might look like curiosity, like they simply want to experience your adventure vicariously. But their interest in your experience contains the heart of civilization itself. Like William Blake's famous poem about holding the world in a grain of sand, when writers show us the world through their eyes, we expand our individual and collective insights into the process of being human.

The Hero's Journey Continues

After the hero returns to the ordinary world, the adventure is finished, allowing the reader to return to his or her own ordinary world. In this final step, the storyteller hands the reins back to the reader.

As successful authors, our journey to "become a writer" is complete. By the end of the journey, we have accepted the role of expert, teacher, or storyteller. And yet, the adventure is not finished. Even after we have achieved our former dreams, we find new ones to draw us ever onward.

YOU ARE THE WRITER WHO LIVES THIS STORY

In your "normal" life, you are relatively private. To become a writer, you must expose yourself to the public, sharing thoughts with people you don't even know. You work diligently, even passionately, to achieve mastery and rise above the obstacles that stand between you and your readers. Finally, you achieve greater skills, compose excellent pieces, and approach your goal. At that point, you discover a new challenge. You must develop an emotional relationship with strangers. To achieve this relationship, you develop the story of yourself as a writer. Finally, as the hero of your story, you earn the right to share your thoughts and images with your global community – your readership.

Become the Author of Your Life Story as a Writer

In your journal, assume the role of a heroic character, and overcome obstacles the way a hero would. Use the following writing prompts to help you face and overcome obstacles.

- I will identify one action that seems to be holding me back today, and instead of interpreting it as an obstacle, I will see it as a step along my path. Then I will take that step. (Write about the obstacle, and how you will step toward and through it.)

- I will diminish the power of a regret or loss by seeing it as an episode that broadens my character. (Write about the loss or regret as if it were the most important lesson you could learn today.)

- I will practice and hone one skill today. (Write about the skill and how you will improve it.)

- Like a hero, I am not alone. I will enlist people to help me on my journey. (Name the person or persons and write what you want to learn from them and how you will work together.)

- In my imagined future as a writer, I visualize the following events and developments. List them.

Act Like a Writer

WRITERS MOVE TENACIOUSLY TOWARD GOALS

In a journal intended only for myself, I wrote anything that came to mind. I never cared if the words were clear or even if they made sense. Like meditation or jogging, the reward was not the end product, but in the activity. After I wrote, I always felt better than when I started. In fact, my most rewarding sessions occurred on bad days. I sat down feeling distraught, lazy, or lonely, knowing I could improve my feelings by pouring my heart onto the page.

When I shifted to writing for others, however, my sessions required concentration. Now, I had to write about a specific topic, and create an article or essay. I had to figure out how to structure the piece, giving it a beginning, middle, and end that would make sense to a reader. And I had to convey the material in interesting sentences and paragraphs.

With this ambitious charter, I found many reasons to avoid my task. "I'm tired." "I'm not in the mood." And the one that I found most convincing: "I don't have time." My reasons for not writing sounded important and real. And yet, if I obeyed them I would never reach my goal. A hero wouldn't quit just because of fatigue or lack of time.

At first, the thought of managing my time seemed wrong. Writing was fun when I loosened the reins and allowed my mind to roam free. But all that freedom was leading me nowhere. I had to solve the paradox – maintain creativity while achieving goals.

In the section *Your Story as a Writer*, you learned how to see yourself as a hero moving tenaciously toward a goal. In this section, you'll learn how to solve seemingly mundane problems like "not enough time," and "I can't focus." As you travel the road from writing for yourself to writing for readers, you will learn to find the time and also stay connected to the wellspring of creative pleasure and self-expression.

WRITING PROMPT

To improve your ability to insert your writing goals into the 24 hours of a day, write journal entries starting with these sentences:

"In some areas of my life, I already use the following time-management techniques to help me do my work."

"Here are some of the ways I could improve my use of time to help accomplish my writing goals."

"As I consider applying time management to my writing, I have the following reservations."

Don't Rebel Against Your "Boss"

As children, we enjoyed the vibrant energy of play. As long as we stayed within our parents' guidelines, we could do anything we wanted. As we grew, our parents adjusted the guidelines to steer us toward adulthood. But eventually we needed to find our own path. During this stage in our lives, our rebellion gave us a sense of power. By pushing away from authority we finally express our true selves.

As we move from rebellious teenager to adulthood, we accept that some rules are valuable, and we submit to them in order to succeed. But when we try to write for readers, we are often influenced by some of the emotional antagonism of rebellion, trying to assert our independence. We might rebel against deadlines or schedules, insisting we need to write anything we want, whenever we want. We might rebel against anyone who tells us we to stick with a schedule, even if we're the ones who are setting it. If you find yourself struggling to follow your own schedule or goals, perhaps you are paying too much attention to your adolescent sense of rebellion.

In the section *Your Story as a Writer*, you reviewed past decisions to weed out obsolete ones. Check to see if your obsolete decisions included one that said, "No one tells me what to do." That cantankerous rule may be blocking the road to success.

WRITING PROMPT

Write about a time when in your life when you rebelled against control.

Write about a time as an adult when you realized that you could express some of that childlike freedom through your words.

Write a scene in which you role-play two parts of yourself. Play the writer in one role and the "boss" in the other. Portray your boss as a compassionate leader who only wants the best for "both of you." Role-play as the writer who realizes that all this instruction and guidance is for your own benefit.

Wandering Attention

Directing attention toward any difficult task requires effort. When you apply that effort, your mind naturally pulls you in other directions. In creative pursuits, this tendency can feel especially compelling. Because we are working voluntarily and can freely walk away from the project anytime we want, we might wander so much we fear that lack of attention is wired into our brains. So many artists complain about their inability to focus, it sometimes seems that ADHD and art go together.

To decide just how pathological your lack of attention really is, consider the focus you bring to bear on a vital or engaging task. For example, do you lose yourself when you prepare the kids for school, or when you play a video game, or are on a phone call with an old friend, or become immersed in a novel? During these activities your attention flows fully in the direction you point it, demonstrating that your mind *is* capable of paying attention. To become a writer, learn how to focus that same degree of attention on your writing goals.

To increase your attention, follow the same advice given to those who suffer from Attention Deficit Hyperactivity Disorder. Treatment for ADHD includes coaching to help you structure your time. You learn tips for making lists, setting priorities, scheduling time, and so on. In fact, ADHD coaching is almost indistinguishable from the advice offered in self-management courses, which increases your efficiency by putting boundaries around your time and tasks. And such techniques don't need to dampen your creative energy – in fact, they provide a safe place in which you can be more creative than ever.

Fear Is a Terrible Taskmaster

When you rely on externally imposed deadlines, your fear of failing supercharges your effort. This may get the job done, but fear is a terrible taskmaster that erodes your self-esteem and burns you out. Fear makes you the slave of external pressure, and takes away the fun.

WRITING PROMPT

> Review your feelings when you are following commands from a person in authority or advice from a mentor. Do you visualize pleasing them, or fear displeasing them? What are the consequences of failure? To what extent are you motivated by competition or proving your worth?

If you are using fear as a motivational tool, wean yourself from it. To improve your long-term prospects, learn to manage yourself through gentle persuasion, time management, and passion to follow your story and fulfill your role. As you form a more effective relationship with time, you will naturally become less dependent on the demoralizing force of fear.

Make Peace with Time

Whether you suffer from a diagnosis or a preference, you can improve your ability to concentrate by practicing. If your mind drifts, bring it back. It sounds trivial, but this habit is worth developing. A high-tech tool called "neurofeedback" teaches you how to adjust your brainwaves into a more relaxed, concentrated stream. Meditation has similar goals without the technology. It helps you let go of distracting thoughts, so your attention flows in the direction you point it. Learning how to intentionally focus your attention is a valuable skill that can improve your quality of life and your ability to complete projects.

You can also increase your ability to focus on your writing by reducing the emotional obstacles that stand in your way. If you feel anxious about the task or are afraid your future readers will not be interested in you, you'll naturally avoid writing. I'll talk about managing your emotions in the section *Think and Feel Like a Writer* and about overcoming fear of your readers in the section *Advanced Audacity*.

HOW TO BREAK THE CYCLE OF INACTION

When you enter a cycle of procrastination, you're like a car stuck in mud. Hitting the gas only seems to dig you in deeper. To escape the trap, learn the difference between actions that dig you in deeper, and those that get you moving forward.

The first ingredient of procrastination is inaction. After you have avoided a task for long enough, your mind adjusts to the current state, and it becomes difficult to see yourself in motion. To break that illusion, redefine your large task into a series of tiny ones. Then perform the first small step. By taking one small step, you regain a sense of forward motion. It becomes easier to take the next one, and the one after that.

To encourage those small steps, create a detailed list. If one action seems too difficult, try something different. When an idea jumps to mind, jot it on a scrap of paper. Go for a walk and speak into a recorder about your story or article. Arrange your notes, find a missing file, brainstorm titles for a piece you want to write, or interview one person. Each step increases your self-confidence and momentum. The most powerful tonic to prevent and cure inaction is the steady trickle of productivity generated by a daily writing habit.

The second ingredient of procrastination is anxiety. A little anxiety is inevitable. You want to excel, learn, and improve. You anticipate the finish line, search for time, worry about success. When you channel your energy toward progress, it helps you focus. When you feel blocked, though, your mind churns, with no discernible results. This wasted energy feels frustrating, and actually increases the anxiety. Once in this state of mind, instead of focusing on progress, you apply your precious energy to self-attacks, worrying about your own failures, frustrations, and fears.

"How could I?" "What is wrong with me?" "I'll never succeed." These doubts imbue the task with an unpleasant agitation. Instead of being fun, the project turns into a chore you'd rather avoid. It's a classic vicious circle. The guiltier you feel, the harder it is to take that first step. Your avoidance makes you feel even guiltier.

You can disengage from the cycle of guilt by replacing guilty, downward-pulling thoughts with positive ones like forgiveness and hope. For example, replace demoralizing statements like "I'll never succeed" with more productive ones like, "I hit a rough patch. Once I get going, I'll be fine." In the section called *Think Like a Writer*, I'll offer techniques to reduce the grip of self-attacking thoughts.

By taking small actions and reducing the grip of anxiety, you will switch from a vicious cycle to a virtuous one that feeds itself, leading you back to productivity.

START YOUR FLOW

Writers have access to a powerful tool to break procrastination: free-writing. When you write the first word, your action opens a gate. Even if you don't feel inspired when you start, writing begins a process, which, through repetition and familiarity, will lead to flow.

If you don't feel inspired, write anyway. Actions that lead you closer to your goals stimulate hope, and hope stimulates inspiration. With practice, you will become adept at choosing actions that improve your state of mind. But to learn how to get moving, don't wait until you feel stuck. Learn techniques right now. Then use them every day to push through the dips and keep your energy flowing.

As the psychologist William James said, "Action seems to follow feeling, but really action and feeling go together; and by regulating the action, which is under the more direct control of the will, we can indirectly regulate the feeling, which is not."

Free-writing and Brainstorming Awaken Your Writing Mind

To write well, you need the gift of written gab. That means you must create as much flow between your mind and your pen as you have between your mind and your mouth. You can awaken this connection by combining the powerful tools of free-writing and brainstorming (also called "clustering"). Free-write to pour your thoughts onto paper. Cluster to generate a variety of insights that spring from your original thought. With practice, these two tools awaken a more fluid connection between the concept or image you wish to communicate and the sentences you record on paper.

Free-writing Taps into Veins of Gold

Do you sit in front of a blank page, unsure of how to fill it, or afraid your language is wooden or filled with mistakes? If you stare too long, the desire for writing passes. Rather than waiting for just the right word, it's best to simply write a first word. To learn how to let words flow freely from your mind on to the page, develop the habit of free-writing.

Free-writing mines your unconscious and your memories, drawing information out of hiding into plain view. The method connects you with your creative center so intimately that it sometimes feels as if you are tapping into your very soul. Free-writing can start anywhere–from something that happened yesterday or that you anticipate happening today – from the name of an old friend. You can even begin your free-writing with the sentence, "I am now free-writing and I don't know what to write."

The most important rule is to set words on paper without comment or judgment. If you find your inner critic speaking up, take steps to appease it. Explain to yourself that this writing is not polished. Don't stop to ponder word choice, grammar, or structure. Consider it to be as private as a diary. You never need to show it to anyone, so your inner critic can take a break.

For more insight into the power of daily free-writing, read the acclaimed book on awakening your creative potential, *The Artist's Way* by Julia Cameron. The foundation of Cameron's method is a free-writing exercise she calls the "Morning Pages." She says, "It is impossible to write 'Morning Pages' for any extended period without coming into contact with an unexpected inner power."

The other classic book on this topic is *Writing Down the Bones* by Natalie Goldberg. Goldberg has devoted her life to offering simple, powerful rules for free-writing. She explains:

> "Keep your hand moving. (Don't pause to reread the line you have just written. That's stalling and trying to get control of what you're saying.)
>
> Don't cross out. (That is editing as you write. Even if you write something you didn't mean to write, leave it.)
>
> Don't worry about spelling, punctuation, grammar. (Don't even care about staying within the margins and lines of the page.)
>
> The aim is to burn through to first thoughts, to the place where energy is unobstructed by social politeness or the internal censor, to the place where you are writing what your mind actually sees and feels, not what it thinks it should see or feel."

When you get into the habit of free-writing regularly, you increase the flow of energy from your creative mind. With your increased ability to transform thoughts into sentences, you can increase the spontaneity of all of your writing. Free-writing can be a complete release, a reverie that opens you to unforeseen possibilities. With such a method, you could go anywhere. Fascinating revelations emerge. Continue to use the free-writing method for years, to enhance flow, to warm up at the start of each journaling session, to reveal details of your emotional landscape, and to build the gift of written gab.

Flow in a Chosen Direction

You can modify the "take me anywhere" method of free-writing by starting with a writing prompt or question. The initial thought starts your mind moving in a particular direction. Once you let yourself go, however, allow your mind to explore freely. You will find yourself learning new aspects of this path that you might never have noticed if you had explored it more methodically. For example, you could ask a question about a character in your story. "I'm Sasha, and I just spotted an old friend across the street. What would I think?" Or, "I need to write about grief. How did I feel the week after my mother died?"

Once you choose a launching point, jump in and let the stream of free-writing carry you. Write for five minutes or set some other specific goal. Write the first word you think of, without evaluating all the other possibilities. Don't censor it. Once you've started writing, don't think about rules or assignments. Don't edit. Don't judge. Don't stop.

You can also free-write to develop your momentum as a writer, to overcome obstacles, recover from setbacks, and build self-confidence. To get the most from this book, use the questions and suggestions in the writing exercises as starting points for free-writing.

Steer your mind gently in the direction of your initial brainstorming, but if your free-writing takes you in a different direction, go with it. Free-writing has enormous value no matter where it takes you, revealing insights, surprising directions, clever turns of phrase. This exercise loosens up your writing "muscles" the way stretching loosens the physical ones.

Clustering – Brainstorm All Over the Page

The human brain is endowed with powerful spatial and visualization skills. We use these natural strengths to help us find our way around town, or to remember where we left the car keys. Fiction writers use visualization to create scenes or whole worlds.

In the late 1970s, author Gabriele Rico wrote her doctoral thesis on a system that harnesses the mind's visualization skills in order to generate ideas. She popularized the method she called "clustering" in her book, *Writing the Natural Way*. Another innovator, Tony Buzan wrote extensively about a similar system he called "mind mapping."

These brainstorming methods allow you to break free from the limitations of thinking along a straight line. Seeing words on paper in this expansive way, you see new associations and juxtapositions that lead to surprising ideas and refreshing word choices.

Start with a blank sheet of paper. At the center of the page, write a word or phrase to evoke a key idea and draw a circle around it. Let your mind roam to related thoughts. Write these elsewhere on the page. Notice the connections and relationships among them.

Circle each new word and draw lines connecting the circles. Some of your ideas spawn new ones. Draw them like spokes radiating from a wheel. Branch far and wide. Have fun. Use colored pens. Visualize connections.

A circle with "I'm stuck" leads to another that says "Super Glue" and the next one says "The time I broke the little ceramic bird" and "It was the only thing my nephew wanted when my mother died." Then you're off and flying with several article ideas: the things we associate with love, the disappointment of death, the first time my nephew and I see our relationship to each other, linked by our love for my mother.

You can use this method at any level of granularity, from trying to find a powerful word to finding the conclusion for an article to finding the theme for your next book. Say you want to write an article about hope. You write the word "hope" in the center of the page. Then you might think of a few things you hope for. You write "oil change before weekend." It has nothing to do with your article, but this is free-brainstorming. No one is grading you for right answers. Then, "The guy who runs the service station seems so decent and hard-working," and then you write, "work generates hope" and "his work generates my hope" and then, "the best way to build hope is to see the good in each other." Now you're starting to see a theme for an article.

Complete this Sentence

Brainstorming can help you find a new way to phrase a sentence, or find a new way to burst through discouragement. Nathaniel Branden in *Six Pillars of Self-Esteem* suggests a method to liberate free advice from its hiding place in your unconscious. Simply write the beginning of a sentence that points you in the right direction. Then mine your unconscious by quickly completing the sentence five times in a row, without thinking. For example:

- To further my writing, today I will …

- To enrich the personality of a character in my article or story I will …

- The real point of the piece I am writing is …

WRITING PROMPT

What big challenge do you wish to resolve? Write your own sentence stubs that point your mind toward the solution. Then use this brainstorming technique to generate answers that flow from your subconscious.

SUSTAIN ENERGETIC WRITING WITH VARIETY

The word "intelligent" evokes the image of high academic achievement. In 1983, psychologist Howard Gardner proposed that humans can be intelligent along a variety of lines, in areas such as music, people, or the way we move our bodies. Gardner's idea, called Multiple Intelligences, has permeated the educational system, helping kids develop other dimensions of themselves beyond "book learning." Writers, too, can benefit from a more expansive view of their mental toolkit.

When you watch someone write, you see the motion of fingers. Not much else seems to be taking place. But inside the writer's mind, all hell is breaking loose. Emotions flow freely, images blaze across the mental movie screen, sounds blare. And the author's verbal imagination is completely engaged in a sublime form of language art that speaks to readers across time and space.

To become a more effective and creative writer, tap into the whole spectrum of your mental capabilities:

- Use your eyes, and other senses
- Vocalize or role play
- Mine your memories for raw material
- Move your body to stir energy and "muscle memory"
- Manage your environment

Use Your Eyes

"Visual thinking" stimulates your right brain and awakens fresh insights that bring your writing to life. You can arouse your visual thinking with a few lines of a doodle, an old photo, or consciously engaging your visual imagination. Whether you are trying to tighten a scene, clearly convey a technical idea, or give unique identity to a character, thinking in pictures can enhance your writing.

DRAW OR DOODLE

Draw your character in a scene. You may object, saying "But I'm not an artist." That's OK. The idea is to stimulate creative thinking. Drawing even rough sketches and stick figures awakens different, nonverbal, creative areas of your brain. A stick figure springing out from behind a tree evokes surprise that brings back a memory and starts your imagination down a new path. You don't need to be limited to concrete events. Drawing an abstract emotion can stimulate your writing, too. Draw the shape of anger. Color it in.

WRITING PROMPT

To gain deeper insight into your essay or story, identify some visual cue that would make the writing come to life. Think of a person, place, or prop. Then draw it, photograph it, video it, or find a photo of it. Use your visual aid to awaken ideas. Free-write for five minutes about what you see.

USE A FEW OF A PICTURE'S THOUSAND WORDS

If a picture is worth a thousand words, skim off a few for your writing. One best-selling author travels to a foreign city, stands at major landmarks and photographs a 360-degree panorama of the area. Later, when he writes, he reviews the photos for visual cues. Memoir writers use photos from their past. If you are writing about a foreign land, look up photos of the place online to stir visual cues.

WRITING PROMPT

What images could help you strengthen a piece you are working on? If you have personal photos handy, review them now. Or find a related image online. Or plan a photo that you could take. With the help of this photographic imagination, describe the time and place.

KNICK KNACKS AND CLOTHES TAKE YOU INTO YOUR CHARACTER'S WORLD

The objects with which we surround ourselves offer clues about taste, family history, and self-image. Wall hangings and knick-knacks represent our taste, favorite vacations, or ancestors. Jewelry and clothing also express our feelings about ourselves. Are room furnishings barren or elaborate, cheap or lavish, carefully planned or slapped together? In your mind's eye, look around. Listing additional objects puts you into the frame of mind of your characters, and will allow readers into that mental state, as well.

WRITING PROMPT

In a passage you are developing, think about the relationship between the people and the objects around them. You can use this exercise in either direction. In a nonfiction piece, think about what the actual objects suggest about the person. In a fiction piece, consider what sort of adornment your character would add to his or her environment.

Use Other Senses

To put yourself and your readers into the scene, conjure up other senses. What smell do you associate with a place you are writing about? When you walked along an outdoor path, the smell might not seem important to you, but it could create a haunting sensual connection for your reader. Did you smell wet autumn leaves, or a whiff from the trash bin or the subtle play of exhaust fumes from the nearby highway? Each smell evokes a specific mood. If you are eating, the tastes might help the reader enter the situation. And taste does not arise only at mealtimes. When a woman stands on a street corner, tears stinging her eyes because her date stood her up again, the mint she popped into her mouth an hour earlier becomes a cruel reminder of her expectations. Tastes can add intensity to fear or anticipation.

Similarly, touch–in all its manifestations–can transport the reader into a scene, including overheated skin on a hot day, tying sandy shoelaces that have been dragging in the mud, and the wind whipping hair into your eyes. Extend the scope of bodily feelings to include your character's biological self-awareness. For example, when he or she feels heart palpitations or a forehead moist with sweat, those sensations convey enormous emotional information.

WRITING PROMPT

> Review a passage you are writing and intensify it by invoking one
> of the senses. To help you enter that state of mind, reproduce
> some aspect of the scene. For example, smell the same thing you
> are writing about.

Vocalize or Role Play

We develop the ability to speak long before we learn to write. If you feel stuck on the written page, return to the source: Engage your vocal cords in the creative process. The act of speaking stimulates parts of your brain that have evolved for sending words to others. And hearing the sound of your own voice activates the brain circuits engaged in receiving words.

READ ALOUD

When you feel stuck on a passage, read it aloud. Simply hearing yourself will give you a fresh perspective. Speak to an imaginary audience, telling a story or trying to convince them of your point of view.

RECORD YOUR IDEAS

Speak your draft ideas into a recorder and then listen to them or transcribe them.

SING

Sing during breaks. This frees up your vocal chords, diaphragm, and chest and moves oxygen through your lungs.

ROLE PLAY CHARACTERS IN YOUR STORY

Get up and move around, acting out one or more characters in your story. Putting your body into the position of your characters and their words into your own voice will give you a fresh perspective.

WRITING PROMPT

Describe specific ways you will use your voice or drama to help free up your flow. When will you use this technique?

Memories Contain a Lifetime of Writing Prompts

Memories provide a rich vein of material. Your mind overflows with sights, sounds, and emotions that you have personally experienced. Snoop around and find insights hidden within scenes of your own life. Also tucked away within your memory are a cast of characters with whom you have shared the stage. Write your impressions of them. What would they think? How did you feel about them?

"What was I thinking in sixth grade when I sat in the orchestra pit, trying to hide behind my French horn while the whole school watched?"

"Describe the slippery fallen leaves as I walked to school in the rain."

Turn memory-writing into a habit. Include sights, sounds, and emotions. By turning your memories into written words, you will not only uncover jewels for your writing, you will develop fascinating insights into your own story.

WRITING PROMPT

To extract nuggets from the goldmine of memory, pick a particular segment of your life. Write about a crush on a teacher. Describe the sound when you closed your locker in high school. What scene does that sound evoke? What did it feel like to climb a rope, or scuff your knee on a hardwood floor during gym class? List the vacations your family took, and pick a time when your whole family laughed. How were you dressed when you opened the door for your first date? When a memory jumps out, get in touch with it by writing keywords on your blank page, and use the clustering technique to link them together. Or, when you see a scene, freewrite. Don't worry about making perfect sense. Just let it flow.

HABITS PREVENT INACTION AND PROMOTE SUCCESS

Suppose you go to bed thinking, "I really ought to write when I wake up tomorrow. I'll set my alarm an hour earlier." When the buzzer sounds, you hit the snooze button and roll over. Finally, feeling guilty, you rouse yourself, prepare a cup of coffee, open your web browser, and read news headlines. Then you look at the clock. "Darn. I've got to get ready for work. Maybe tomorrow."

These low-energy sessions suck away your time as well as your ambition. When you approach your tasks on this case-by-case basis, you wrestle with willpower each time. The antidote is not more willpower. Instead, apply your time and effort to forming a habit. Once the habit is formed, instead of dragging yourself reluctantly to your chair, your routine will propel you with such vigor that you are mentally crafting sentences before you even sit down.

Habits were praised in ancient times as the key to good character. In modern times, habits have fallen out of favor. That's too bad, because without attention to the way we create and form habits, we are often at their mercy. To become a writer, learn the power and importance of habits. And then, instead of wrestling with your willpower for each individual writing session, apply effort to developing and maintaining a regular writing routine.

If you still think you write best when you are "in the mood," you will be delighted to discover that habits not only get you to the desk, but also create a mental state in which your flow can flourish.

When you first form the habit, you must overcome familiar reluctance and inner debates. But you have a new long-term motivation for pushing through resistance. Once you establish the pattern, it will provide an inner compulsion that will improve your productivity for years to come.

Establish your habit the way you propelled a swing when you were a child. Start with the smallest push. Then pump your legs at just the right moment to urge the swing a little farther each time. With a small amount of energy added to each cycle, before long you are flying high and can sustain this exhilarating flight with hardly any added effort.

Once it's firmly inserted into your program, it becomes as automatic as brushing your teeth. Write every day, automatically, without needing to think about or plan for it.

Some Habits are Easier to Start than Others

At first, simple activities might seem to be the ones most likely to induce a feeling of flow. Mihaly Csikszentmihalyi (pronounced "chick-sent-me-high"), however, who spent a lifetime studying the flow state, observed that a high degree of challenge is required in order to feel deep satisfaction. For example, if you were to eat an ice cream cone, the complexity of the action is low and the satisfaction is correspondingly brief. It's easy to become habituated to such low-energy activities. Watching television or eating and drinking too much are activities we often associate with the word "habit."

There are also good habits. The successful runner, pianist, writer, scientist, or business person all feel compelled to follow their long-term goals, even when the daily work required to achieving them is difficult. Despite the degree of difficulty, people who engage in such highly-structured activities experience as much pleasure as the ice cream eaters, but over a different time span.

People who successfully achieve difficult accomplishments spend years building these habits into their daily routines. Once these apparently-difficult activities have become habits, missing a scheduled session causes agitation or longing. Day after day, season after season, year after year, they improve their expertise and acquire valuable experience. They gather social networks that offer emotional as well as technical support. Gradually these long-term pursuits pay back with long-term rewards, including money, social stature, and personal fulfillment.

When you were a child, your parents encouraged you to learn difficult skills. When you grew up, your boss or the demands of customers took over, expecting you to perform up to their standards. However, the pressure to write a novel, article, or essay comes from motivation you muster from within yourself. You push yourself toward excellence, sign up for groups and classes, and strategize to reach readers. And you must choose these activities over all the other things you could do with your time. It's easier to go for a walk, read a book, or do anything other than write. Despite these convenient options, your longing nags at you. You hope that once you're in the habit, you will no longer need to fight with your excuses. The habit will drag you to the desk again and again.

Routine Activities that Help Writers

Successful writers don't wait until they are in the mood to write. They harness the power of habits; for example, they set a minimum amount of time in the chair or number of pages completed. To write successfully, find a routine that will carry you toward your goals. Here are some of the regular activities that can help you succeed.

FREE-WRITE

As discussed earlier, free-writing liberates the flow of words from mind to page. Free-writing unearths gems, strengthens your writing "legs," and gets you into the chair. As you become more comfortable with this activity, you will be able to set yourself in motion toward a goal, and then let your mind loose to follow that path.

EDIT AND CRITIQUE

To write effectively, you need to edit effectively. Editing, like other skills, improves with practice. To practice, get into the habit of reviewing your own drafts, and mark them up as if you were an editor. Learn even more by joining a critique group. In such a group, you will have the opportunity to edit other people's work as well as receive their edits of yours.

FOCUS ON MOVING PROJECTS FROM PRIVATE TO PUBLIC

To reach readers, you face a set of challenges that is very different from sitting in your chair in a writing flow. You must decide who will like this piece, and then reach toward them. Like any difficult task, the power of habits can make the climb easier. For example, regularly look for the people who will publish or read your work, and then contact them. By building outreach into your routine, you acquire a rhythm that helps you overcome resistance and builds momentum and enthusiasm.

MANAGE YOUR TIME

To manage your time effectively, form the habit of prioritizing tasks and following a to-do list. Planning can help you maintain your writing tasks amid all the other responsibilities of life. You only have 24 hours each day. Habits help you use them wisely.

WORK HABITS

Once you sit at your desk and begin to write, your choices disappear and you enter the zone. That is a great place to be, but you also need to respond to times when you are not in that zone. Your thoughts and actions between writing sessions could replenish your energy and set up the next round of flow. Instead of scrambling for a new strategy each time you slow down, develop an awareness of what works and what doesn't, and then regularly and persistently follow the path toward energetic writing.

REPLACE DRAINING LIFESTYLE PATTERNS

Once you establish a habit, it triggers primal circuits in your brain that make it feel important – even urgent. As a result, simple activities like watching television may become more important than achieving your dreams. Once you appreciate the power of habits, you can plan accordingly. Reduce activities that leave you feeling empty, and replace them with energizing ones.

IMPROVE THOUGHTS THAT INFLUENCE MOOD

Many of the thoughts that influence mood arise automatically from old patterns. For example, when things don't go your way, you may mutter, "Life stinks. I'll never succeed." Such mental habits have a powerful impact on energy. Self-doubt and worry stifle our creative endowment. To recover this valuable energy, take advantage of research that consistently shows that consciously influencing our thoughts affects our mood. With training, you can get into the habit of thinking more uplifting thoughts. You'll learn about thought habits in the section called *Think and Feel Like a Writer*.

Habit Forming: A Step-by-Step Guide

To learn more about starting a habit, consider the observations made by psychologist James Prochaska, who has years of clinical research to help smokers stop smoking. By carefully observing his subjects, he developed methods that help people start, stop and change their habits. He explains his observations and system in the book *Changing for Good*. I have adapted the steps in Prochaska's method to help you increase your chances of successfully forming and maintaining writing habits.

Start your planning by keeping a journal where you can record information and insights about your habit. The information you gather at the beginning will help you focus your energy, develop strategies, and overcome obstacles.

1) IDENTIFY A DESIRABLE BEHAVIOR

Writers have a number of important tasks. We must generate ideas, create first drafts, revise, get feedback, and send our work to readers. All of these larger activities can benefit from habits. The important challenge for every writer is to develop the habits that lead to success. Your first job is to find the ones that you need, and then develop them. Work on one at a time, so you are not overwhelmed by this important step. To build a foundation, follow Julia Cameron's suggestion and free-write for fifteen minutes every morning. Free-writing stimulates the dance between your creative conscious and unconscious mind.

Other examples:

- Write four pages of your manuscript every day

- Keep a pipeline of six essays and finish one each week

- Find and follow a routine that bumps you past slumps

- Develop and follow self-talk habits that maintain energy

WRITING PROMPT

What type of habit will help you fulfill your goals? Free-writing? Drafting your book? Outlining? Sending out queries to editors or agents?

2) RESEARCH YOUR HABIT

This is your time to gather resources and energy. Write strategies and vows in your habit-change journal. To find out how other people overcome their obstacles, read books about writing habits. Interview fellow writers to learn about their daily writing habits.

Review your available time, and plan where this habit will fit into your life. If you foresee issues relating to your sleep or work schedule, develop a sub-plan just to solve those issues. To write early in the morning, you may need to go to bed earlier. If you find it too easy to hit the snooze button and roll over for more sleep, find a more effective alarm clock. The gentlest one I've found glows with light a few minutes before buzzing. Or move your alarm to the other side of the room. In addition to time, consider your place. You may also need to organize your computer files or your desk.

Before you start your habit in earnest, experiment. Do it a few times, to get a feel for it and to identify any additional issues.

3) LIST BENEFITS OF YOUR HABIT

Your desire will fuel your determination, so develop a thorough list of your reasons for incorporating writing into a daily routine. Identify clear compelling reasons for developing the habit, so when you need a boost, you can return to the list. Become eloquent in the expression of your passion to be a writer.

For example, here are some of mine. By writing every day, I:

- Sustain forward momentum on my projects

- Increase my sense of connection with my writing and contribute to my identity as "a writer"

- Stir creativity so ideas float toward me when I'm taking a shower, meditating, or going for a walk

- Feel centered and confident to face the rest of the day

- Discover insights that surprise, inform, and lift me

WRITING PROMPT

Write your reasons as clearly and compellingly as possible. By writing your motivations now, you provide energy later. What do you want to accomplish? How is this habit going to help you achieve your goal? What is the penalty of failing to achieve your goal? What inconveniences and discomforts are you willing to put up with to achieve your goal?

4) PLAN TO OVERCOME OBJECTIONS

Develop strategies for overcoming obstacles. With adequate preparation, you can reduce the severity of obstacles or eliminate them altogether, before you even start your habit. The strategies you come up with during this step will sustain you when you feel like quitting.

Here are suggestions to reduce obstacles before they arise:

- Don't wait until your family notices you writing. Discuss it with them from the beginning. Address their concerns, if any. Create a list of benefits for them. Tell them it will make you happier and they'll be proud to see your name in print.

- Buy additional bright lights to set up around your desk. Good lighting makes it easier to see and boosts your energy.

- Tool up to wake up. Buy a glow light alarm, or set your lamp on a timer. Place a second alarm clock on the other side of the room. Light plus sound will wake you more effectively than either one alone.

- Instead of staying up late to watch your favorite show, plan to record it and watch it early the next evening.

Some obstacles will be generated by your own mind. For example, you may tell yourself "Not today" or "I'm not in the mood." Such objections sound silly when you are filled with resolve, but they sound important when you're tired. To get through those moments, consider in advance what you can say to yourself to refute these objections.

For example, anticipate thoughts that may run through your mind when you hear the alarm clock. Instead of letting these stay-in-bed statements have their way with you, create a repertoire of positive motivational statements, write them on index cards, and rehearse them.

- In answer to "Maybe tomorrow," you could say, "Today is yesterday's tomorrow."

- In answer to "I don't have time" you could say "This is important to me. I will make time."

I'll talk more about the importance of thoughts in the section called *Think Like a Writer*. When you are ready to take a stand against draining and demoralizing thoughts, you might want to develop a plan to help you substitute encouraging thoughts in place of the ones that try to slow you down.

5) FORM A DETAILED PLAN

A good plan establishes orderly expectations and provides a container within which your writing can flow. By deciding in advance which direction you want to go and how to get there, you can reduce distractions and fulfill promises.

Write your plan in your habit-change journal or file. If you need to perform preliminary actions like buying materials or organizing your desk, put these on your list, too.

- Define exactly what times you will write. For example, to get up at 6:00 AM and get enough sleep, plan when you'll need to go to bed.

- If you intend to write on paper, prepare your writing pad. If you intend to use a computer, decide in advance how you will save your files.

- Talk to a friend who already writes in the morning and agree on a mutual support/accountability system.

6) EXECUTE THE PLAN

By now you know what you want to achieve. You have acknowledged the complexity of the task, and have poured energy into your plan. You have supports, you have knowledge, and each time you do your habit you gather experience. Here are some things to remember:

- Before your habit has taken hold, routine writing may seem like drudgery. At this stage, you must push through the temptation to only write when you are in the mood. Use social supports, motivational statements, responses to your objections, and all the other techniques and plans you have prepared. Over time, your writing habit will form a groove that will be easier follow. Your habit itself will create the mood.

- Remember your motivations. Visualize images of success, longings to tell your story, and other motivations. It could take you years to accomplish your goals so you need to think about your long-term relationship to writing. By building these habits and then persistently following them, you are crafting a life that leads toward your dreams.

- Start each session with fun writing exercises to pull yourself into the flow. For example, post a writing prompt at your desk before you go to sleep and in the morning, spend the first five minutes free-writing to answer that prompt. Bring beauty, comfort, and energy to your desk. Associate as much pleasure as possible with your writing task, and reduce dread of all kinds.

- Weekends or vacations might seem to provide valid exemptions from your writing habit. Remember, though, that adhering to the routine whenever possible will make it stronger. In fact, regular writing can itself provide an anchor that steadies you through the storms of change. Over time, you see your writing as part of your self-image, rather than an intrusion.

7) MAINTENANCE: KEEP GOING

After you've continued your habit for a while, you will enjoy the automatic impulse to achieve your task. However, some effort is required to maintain your habit. Stay alert for disruptions. If circumstances or moods knock you off your habit, get back on and keep going. Here are additional suggestions for sticking to or renewing your routine.

- Look at each day's writing not just as the fulfillment of an obligation but also as a contribution to the productivity of every day in the future.

- Review your long-term goals and allow them to stir up emotions of desire for a more creative direction.

- Reach out to the supports you established during your planning stage.

- Look back and appreciate your achievements. Praise yourself for them and remind yourself that small steps add up to progress.

- If you slip, don't beat yourself up. Guilt makes you feel weak and incompetent. Instead, use the strategy touted by motivational leaders: *If you want someone to do a good job, praise him for the one he is already doing.* Praise yourself for every victory, large and small. Even congratulate yourself for good intentions. Avoid guilt, and build confidence. As soon as you are ready, renew your effort, taking advantage of all the good planning and experience you have already invested.

Now Plan Your Own Writing Habit

To implement a habit, follow a habit-change plan. As you incorporate your new behavior into your routine, it becomes part of the pattern that carries you, step by step, closer to your dreams. Writing every day contributes to skills and productivity. Because you are in the flow, you spend little of your time wondering *if* you should write, and more of your time actually writing.

Emergencies might interfere with your habit, or your resolve might erode over time. As soon as possible, review your plan, and either return to it or revise the plan.

As you develop the knack of forming and changing your habits, you gain great power over other aspects of your life. You can manage your impulses, your time, and your actions more effectively.

Change a Habit, Change a Life

In each moment, we make choices and then act. Hopefully, these actions are meaningful enough to satisfy us by the end of each day. And beyond the satisfaction of each day, we aspire to the cumulative effect of our actions through time. Each moment, each day, week, month, and year, our actions add up. Habits provide the best opportunity to influence this cumulative effect. Through repetition, small things become great. To achieve our dreams, we need to construct the habits that will lead us where we want to go.

EXPAND YOUR CHOICES, AND THEN ACT

Our joy of self-expression reaches a crescendo when we're in a state of flow, writing with effortless speed, as if we were running down a mountain, and at the same time, feeling like we are reaching an ever-higher vantage point. At such times, we feel like observers of a process, or recipients of a gift. We hang onto these moments and treasure them. These are moments worth living for. But successful writers don't sit back and wait for these moments to happen.

Writers write, over and over, every day, despite obstacles. To do so, they plan and then diligently follow the plan. They manage time while maintaining flexibility so their creativity dances in the spaces between freedom and control

As writers, we tap into one of the most marvelous tools for maintaining this balance: our own writing. Writing opens us to fresh descriptions, insights, and images. We express powerful feelings in new ways, and through our words experience the exhilarating freedom hidden within our otherwise structured lives.

Just as a poet creates profound emotions within the confinement of a stanza, a painter turns a blank canvas into a visionary window, and a playwright portrays tension and resolution on a stage just a few yards long and wide, we learn to express our dreams by sitting still and crafting words. Our 24-hour day is the stanza, the canvas, the stage, within which we craft the story of our writing success.

When you work hard, creatively, and wisely, your effort will bring you closer to flight, and when the breeze of the muse flows, it lifts you higher. Even with excellent planning and a commitment to place yourself on the path to inspiration, however, your mind can drag you down. "I want to sleep in." "I don't feel like writing today." "Just this one day doesn't really matter."

Your own objections block the good things you want to do. Each objection sounds logical and stifles your effort. By delving into the interior world of your own mental objections, you can apply adult wisdom to answering these objections and continuing toward your goals.

Think and Feel Like a Writer

IN SEARCH OF THE WRITING STATE OF MIND

Imagine waking from a vivid dream. You still see brilliant scenes and clever characters so real you feel you could touch them. You race to your keyboard, where descriptions flow from your fingers as fast as you can type. You barely notice your body. After an hour, you can no longer ignore your other responsibilities. Reluctantly you tear yourself away.

Circumstances prevent you from returning, and a few days later you drag yourself to your writing table. Your words look like someone else's. Your mind wanders toward snacks and chores. You think, "Now I'll never finish this story. If only I didn't stop."

Your writing differs so drastically from one session to another, not because of a change in talent or available time but because of your state of mind. States of mind have an enormous influence over our ability to write. One moment you are relaxed, and roll with the punches. Another time, you feel tense and overreact to every annoyance.

Some aspiring writers believe that since their best writing occurs during inspired states of mind, all they need to do is wait for such states to appear, and then words will pour forth like jewels. It's dangerous to wait for such states of mind. If you are willing to write only when you are "in the mood," you could begin to feel stagnant and helpless, taking you ever further away from productivity.

Don't wait for the right mood. Become an active participant in authoring your state of mind. To avoid slumps altogether, form habits. When you are in a writing habit, your mental state is swept up into the daily motion toward your goals. Steven Pressfield, in his book *The War of Art*, advises how to overcome the resistance to write:

> "Someone once asked Somerset Maugham if he wrote on a schedule or only when struck by inspiration. 'I write only when inspiration strikes,' he replied. 'Fortunately it strikes every morning at nine o'clock sharp.' … Maugham … set in motion a mysterious but infallible sequence of events that would produce inspiration as surely as if the goddess had synchronized her watch with his."

Before your habit is firmly established, however, you must develop strategies to maintain momentum through rough patches. What can you do when you are sitting there, and the effort doesn't seem worth it? Nothing is flowing. You think, "What's the use?"

Without any strategies to help you manage your thoughts and feelings, you could react to slowdowns in a self-destructive way, accusing yourself of laziness, weak will, or lack of talent. You think "just do it" like a mantra, spending more hours staring at a blank screen. You might turn your frustration against other people, scorning those who have succeeded, or blaming gatekeepers. Not only is this wasted time and energy, it's counterproductive. Griping makes you feel bad without moving you closer to your goals.

If you have not been successful at improving your state of mind, reevaluate your strategies and find better ones. The key to productive writing requires a holistic approach that includes both the activity of writing as well as the mood you are in when you show up. Turn toward your own state of mind, and attempt to improve the mental energy and clarity you bring to the task.

Moods often seem to be dictated by external circumstances. Sunny skies or recent praise makes you feel cheerful. When stuck in traffic or after receiving a late penalty from the credit card company, you feel agitated. Moods can be driven by an awakened memory, or even by a fictional story. We go to the movies and pay money to allow the actors to take our emotions for a ride.

The fact that your mood can shift so quickly hints at a sublime fact of life: *You don't need to be stuck in an undesirable state of mind.* Psychologists have been teaching since the mid-twentieth century that our feelings result not from external events but from internal reactions. These modern thinkers weren't the first to notice. Albert Ellis, one of the founders of Cognitive Psychology often quoted the Greek philosopher Epictetus, who 2,000 years ago said, "Men are disturbed not by things, but by the view which they take of them." In other words, we can't always control events, but we can do our best to influence our own response.

CARE FOR THE WRITER'S MIND

After attending a classical piano recital performed by Temple University music students, I asked my friend why so many of the young people in the audience were wearing scarves around their necks. She smiled. "Those are the singing majors. That's how they protect their instruments." I loved that image of protecting the part of themselves that made beautiful music. Writers too, have instruments to protect: To focus productively and creatively on the task, we must care for our moods and thoughts.

Once you get into the flow, writing itself energizes you, but if you feel depleted, you may not be able to start. To achieve your writing goals, keep your emotional state whole and healthy.

Imagine

An often-used psychological technique for helping sufferers of fear and anxiety is to teach them to create an imagined "safe place." By inventing or remembering a comforting place, you can "travel" there in your imagination when you feel threatened or overwhelmed. Press this method into the service of your writing goals by visualizing the perfect place where you could construct your stories or other pieces. For example, I remember an idyllic vacation on a Caribbean Island under a cabana, enjoying the heat, the breeze off the ocean, the expanse of sand, and the relaxing presence of my family. To this image, I add a writer's notebook, a good pen and a comfortable beach chair and I visualize myself composing sentences and stories.

VISUALIZATION PROMPT

> Describe a scene that you either remember or imagine, where you could maintain an almost magical connection with your craft.

Move

According to self-help guru Tony Robbins, physical activity can have an enormous impact on your mental state and will give you many of the same results as a pep talk. He says, "Motion Equals Emotion." Robbins demonstrates this invigorating effect during his all-day workshops, energizing his audience by getting them to stand and jump to high-energy music. You could try a similar exercise yourself.

When your brain shuts down, stand up. Turn on the music and dance for a few minutes. Stretch. Do calisthenics. Pace the room or walk on a treadmill and let thoughts flow through your mind. When an idea occurs, jot it down or speak into a recorder.

By moving around, you change your state of mind and jolt yourself out of bottom-of-brain thinking. Movement sends blood to your brain and shakes stagnation out of your mind. It's almost impossible to feel sluggish when you're jumping around. In motion you become a pioneer, a researcher, a revolutionary. When the impulse to move has passed, and you feel yourself pulled into the writing flow, sit down and continue from where you left off.

When I need a fresh perspective, I go for a walk on the treadmill. With a notebook propped in front of me for notes and edits, I can develop ideas more energetically than when sitting still. I also use my voice on the treadmill, speaking my ideas into a recorder or to the empty room.

In addition to moving as a way to shift your energy during writing sessions, build regular movement into your self-care program. Research shows that exercise as simple as a regular walk decreases depression and stimulates brain-cell development, so after a walk, you'll be both happier and smarter.

RELAX YOUR MUSCLES

When you sit in the same position for an extended period, muscles become tense. Tense muscles in your neck and head can cause headaches. Tense muscles in your chest, shoulders, and diaphragm stifle your breathing, making you feel bad all over.

Relieve tension by consciously scanning your body. Release the tension from face, neck, and shoulders. Relax the muscles in your chest and upper back to free your breathing. When your breathing is relaxed and full, your whole body will assist you in your flow.

Relax your eyes, occasionally, too. Look softly into the distance, focusing on nothing in particular. Without turning your head or moving your eyes, become aware of what lies in the periphery.

WRITING PROMPT

In the section *Act Like a Writer,* I talked about forming habits that promote your writing. In addition to writing activities, also consider habits that add to or detract from the health of your "instrument." Look for an Achilles' heel, a weak spot, in your routine. What activity that you now regularly engage in might be stealing your time and energy? How does this activity make you feel, in the hour you do it, or over a period of years?

To become more conscious of habits, keep a log. For the next week, record the time that goes toward this activity. As you recognize an energy-draining habit, write a plan that will replace it with a more energizing one.

Sculpt Your Writing Environment

When you're in an ultra-focused state, you are completely absorbed in your writing and oblivious to your surroundings. Most of us, though, most of the time, are influenced by our environment. The actual influence of environment varies enormously from one writer to the next and even one part of the day to the next. Some writers work best at a food court in the mall, while others need an uncluttered office with absolute silence. Become aware of your environment and experiment to find what works best for you.

EXPERIMENT WITH SOUNDS AND SILENCE

The sounds around you have a powerful, unconscious effect. Experiment to see what work best Some writers prefer silence. White noise blocks out distractions. For example, a fan, electronic babbling brook, or a desktop fountain could influence the ease with which you enter a flow state. Or explore musical genres to see how they affect your writing mood. Try different sounds for free-writing versus editing.

Many writers feel most creative in a crowd, sitting at the coffee shop and feeling somehow simultaneously soothed and stimulated by the hubbub, the conversations just out of earshot, the background music, and people coming and going.

CREATE A COMFORTING SPACE

Arrange your lights, books, and computer to be more comfortable. Decorate with photographs. Reduce clutter. Is your chair comfortable? You want your writing desk to call to you, so improving the quality of your chair could propel you toward writing success!

USE YOUR DESK JUST FOR WRITING.

Pay bills somewhere else.

OBSERVATIONS THAT SLIP THROUGH THE CRACKS IN TIME

Keep a notebook or recorder handy and record thoughts at a stop light, a restaurant, or anywhere you happen to be when a thought hits you. Insights delivered by your unconscious while you aren't paying attention stimulate great writing back at your desk.

WRITING PROMPT

Describe specific ways you can manage your environment to free up your flow. How and when will you use these techniques?

Read

To care for your writing mind, read books. Reading serves us in a variety of ways. Books about writing provide instruction and inspiration. And learning from others through the printed word is one of the foundations of civilization. The writers who came before you offered their observations and wisdom. As a writer, you will absorb their worldviews. Then embellished and modified by your own unique perspective and life experience, you'll pass on an updated form to your own readers.

Sol Stein in *Stein on Writing* makes an interesting observation about the relationship between what writers read and what they sell. "I have never witnessed . . . a writer's work succeeding notably in a field he doesn't habitually read for pleasure."

Befriend Your Unconscious

When we are in a creative flow, the words emanate from a source that seems wiser and deeper than our conscious mental process. This deep pool has been revered by artists throughout the ages. Tapping into this source feels like finding treasure within your own mind, revealing nuance, insight and compelling phrase. But the timetable that opens and closes the doorway seems outside our conscious control. While you can't force this state of mind, you can cultivate your relationship with it.

MEDITATE

During meditation, you stop analyzing and correcting your thought patterns. Instead, you attempt to look past them. Like the advice to star-gazers that to see a star you shouldn't look directly at it, when you meditate, you should direct your attention away from daily responsibilities. This allows you to become more attuned to your unconscious energy. Like physical exercise, meditation is most effective when done regularly.

JOURNALING IMPROVES YOUR MOOD

At the top of the human brain lies the enormous prefrontal cortex, far larger, per body weight than that of most other mammals. The prefrontal cortex is responsible for complex planning, decision-making, and adjusting behavior to conform to society's rules. Like an orchestra leader synchronizing the discordant sounds of individual instruments, the top of the brain helps direct the disparate influences of all the other parts. You can improve the health and influence of your top-of-brain by improving your relationship with words.

Becoming more comfortable with your verbal explanations helps you understand better who you are and what you want to become. As you write, you bring ideas and emotions into conscious attention, giving you the opportunity to process them in the light of your wisdom, converting yourself from a victim of your thoughts into an active participant.

It's hard to write when you feel miserable. One of the best ways to pick up your mood is to write in your journal. Research by James Pennebaker at the University of Texas supports that circular reasoning. The act of writing makes it easier and more fun to write.

Pennebaker's research shows that pouring your heart into your journal improves mood and even health. Many journal writers and journal writing advocates, including me, have found that journal writing supplements psychotherapy and self-help programs, accelerating insights that help make sense of your inner landscape. Writing helps free you from stuck emotions left over from times when events piled up too fast to explain. Now, looking back on those events, you can reframe your experiences in a light that makes more sense.

Neurological imaging reveals that in your search to express yourself in words, you are generating pleasurable sensations in your brain. And as your words flow, the muse occasionally breezes by. Her unique turn of phrase, image, or insight provides you with a glimpse of her presence in your life. Routine writing sessions create a sort of psychic harbor, a home base, to shelter you through slumps, through travel to uncomfortable places, or through changes that shake your self-confidence

If Depression Drags You Down

The meaning of the word "depression" has changed over the decades. Until the middle of the twentieth century, it implied a sense of melancholy, caused, for example, by unrequited love or the loss of a loved one. In recent times, the word indicates a condition in which sadness is only one symptom. You may also feel:

- No get-up-and-go
- Unable to pursue goals
- Easily discouraged
- Sleepy

Such feelings are death for a writer who is staring at a blank page. If you suffer from these general symptoms, then relieving the symptoms could be an important step toward success.

Along with the modern definition of depression come a number of solutions, including the main ones, talk therapy and medication. Talking to a therapist relieves mental pressure and provides insight that can help you get back into gear. Anti-depressant medications tweak your brain chemistry to improve energy and a sense of self-worth. Research consistently shows that talk therapy is about as good as medication for relieving depression, and that a combination of talk therapy and medication relieves depression better than either one alone. Research also supports the positive effects of exercise, meditation, journaling, and light therapy.

Reduce the Distraction of Anxiety

Agitated feelings make it harder to work. We can be stirred up by fear, helplessness, relationship issues, loneliness . . . the list is endless. Sometimes our writing helps relieve these feelings. Other times, the feelings interfere with our writing. If you feel anxiety is interfering with your goals, then relieving that distraction can help.

When we call a situation "stressful," we blur the line between external events and internal reactions. The word "stressful" implies the relentless pressures of external circumstances of bills, health, family, and job. But more accurately, "stress" describes our internal response to the events. The pressure seems to enter into our body and stay there. Our mind and muscles feel tense. We are more easily angered, frustrated, or depressed. Stress even impairs our immune system.

While negative circumstances may be unavoidable, we have some control over the way we react. By improving our skill at coping with pressure, we put ourselves in the best frame of mind to focus on creativity, despite difficult situations.

TALK BACK TO AUTOMATIC THOUGHTS

As writers, we strive to use words that exert power over readers. We want our words to entice them, please them, and incite emotional reactions within them. However, we are not nearly so focused on the influence words have on ourselves. Our thoughts have a surprisingly strong affect over our ability to achieve our goals. In this section, I show you how to modify those thoughts.

When you think about your writing, enthusiastic, courageous thoughts propel you forward. Mixed in with the good thoughts are negatively charged phrases. Doubts like "I'm not good enough" or "this will never succeed" seem innocuous. And yet, they stir up disturbing emotions that pull your attention to the bottom of your brain, shifting your state of mind from creativity to self-defense.

A method called Cognitive Therapy emerged in the 1950s and has gained credibility since then, thanks to research, and the practical experience of thousands of trained psychotherapists who helped clients improve their feelings by changing their thoughts. The method entered the mainstream in 1980, thanks to a bestselling book by David Burns called *Feeling Good*.

The research shows how common it is for people to criticize themselves and tear themselves down, and how such apparently innocuous self-attacks can drain energy. Cognitive Therapy can help writers who routinely criticize themselves, or say rude things about their own abilities.

Extensive research has demonstrated that counteracting such thoughts helps maintain an upbeat, practical, energized state of mind. Writers have a head start on this method, since we are familiar with the importance of finding the right word.

REPLACE WORRIES WITH OPTIMISM, SUPPORT, AND PLANS

At first it may feel awkward to adjust the nuances of what goes on inside your own mind, but over time, you learn to hear and adjust your self-talk. By fine-tuning the subtleties of what you say to yourself, you reduce anxiety and depression, quiet the inner critic, and put yourself into a more creative frame of mind. And you will find more energy to promote your work to editors and readers.

When you first try to change the way you think, the task might seem impossible, like sitting at a piano and attempting to play a sonata before you can play scales. Like any new skill, you have to learn it in steps. Use your left brain's ability to analyze the problem and create a plan. Then practice each step. Learning a new skill often feels like drudgery, as it requires drills and beginner mistakes. But once you incorporate the activity into your routine, the right brain takes over, allowing you to perform the behavior with far less effort.

In the section, *Act Like a Writer*, I provided the steps to form a writing habit. Review that procedure and apply it to thinking. First, identify the problem, then find the solution. Make an emotional commitment to the solution, and overcome internal objections. Plan the steps, and then apply your energy to achieving each step. Over time, your practice will turn the new activity into an old habit.

LIST THE BENEFITS

You can overcome draining and distracting emotions by changing the thoughts that block the path. To develop the mental habits of a successful writer, shift your thoughts from discouragement to courage, from depression to hope. Here is how Cognitive Therapy achieves these goals.

- The method reduces self-attack and increases self-support.

- Once you learn to listen carefully to automatic thoughts, you discover that the first thought is not always the most accurate one. By allowing yourself to explore your thoughts, you expand your emotional options.

- By inserting wisdom into your thoughts, you overcome mental habits that were hurting your best long-term interests.

OVERCOME OBJECTIONS

How do you feel about thinking about thinking? (Yes, I am inviting you to think about thinking about thinking.) If the prospect makes you nervous, you're not alone. I certainly felt uncomfortable when I first tried it. I had no idea I could talk back to my own thought stream, and I wasn't sure I wanted to try. Finally, I relented.

From the first self-affirming statement I saw value. Gradually, I decided that this system was smarter and more natural than allowing my thoughts to run automatically without conscious intervention.

To take advantage of this system, consider your own attitudes. Here are some of the objections people raise about modifying their own automatic thoughts:

- "Thoughts rush through so fast and furious, I'm unable to change them."

- "Once I start thinking about thoughts, I'm afraid I'll get lost."

- "I don't know what to say instead."

- "Negative thoughts are more sophisticated and true than positive ones."

- "Thinking about thinking seems really weird."

When preparing to embark on this process, overcome these objections by reading the rest of this section and trying some of the methods. For a more extensive explanation, read the best-selling book *The Feeling Good Handbook*, by Dr. David Burns. Consider the many benefits the method offers, and find out which strategies work best for you.

We all manage our self-talk to some extent. For example, many free-writing teachers promote the notion of "talking back to your inner critic." When you tell your inner critic to leave you alone, you are already using self-talk. Cognitive therapy extends that advice and adds other methods to help you modify your inner dialogue.

Once you get in touch with your inner dialogue, you will be in a better position to appreciate the benefits of Cognitive Therapy. But if you fear some less-enlightened individuals might doubt your sanity, keep your self-talk a secret. Or better yet, go ahead and doubt *their* sanity. By *not* paying conscious attention to their own thoughts, they surrender themselves to their automatic thinking. You, on the other hand, are willing to explore other options. As a writer, you rely on this conscious attention to words. In fact, as a writer, freedom of thought is one of your most valuable assets.

Perhaps your inner critic feels threatened by your interest in positive thinking. She fears that if you learn how to talk back to her, you might no longer listen to her. Tell this inner critic that your thoughts are your business and you will think anything you want. Or better yet, rather than start an argument with your inner critic, speak soothingly to her the way you would talk to an edgy friend. "Look. It's OK. We're going to work this out together. We both want the same thing–excellent, energetic writing. Instead of fighting about it, let's work as a team."

First Steps: How to Become Aware of Self-talk

Talking back to your automatic thoughts requires that you first must be able to hear them. This might be a new skill for you, since so few of our parents or teachers coached us on this self-awareness.

Writers have a head start in the skill of hearing our own thoughts. We do it all the time. Whenever we write or edit a sentence, we are listening to words in our mind. During free-writing, we watch self-talk appear on the page. Writers not only *know* about the presence of self-talk. We *rely* on it.

Meditators also foster a conscious awareness of their own thought stream. This awareness arises from a paradox. Many forms of meditation advise us to sit for a period of time and *ignore* our self-talk. When we attempt to ignore our thoughts, we become increasingly aware of them.

Here is a summary of methods that help you become more aware of the patterns of your thinking:

- During free-writing, thoughts jump into plain sight. Free-writing allows you to see and hear your thoughts.
- Talk therapy helps you explore the influence your thoughts have on your feelings.
- During meditation, while you are attempting to "let your thoughts go," you become increasingly aware of the presence of thoughts flowing through your mind.
- Books about positive thinking and cognitive therapy teach you to listen to and adjust your thoughts.

Introduction to Improving Your Self-Talk

To influence the thoughts that move you toward or away from your writing goals, study this short list of skewed or "distorted" thoughts that can get you into a mental bind, followed by suggestions for easing your thoughts in a more positive direction.

- Generalizations
- Labels
- Demoralizing comparisons
- All-or-nothing thinking
- Shoulding yourself
- Worry about the future or "crystal-ball gazing"

Generalizations: "I always quit" or "I never do it right"

When you're frustrated with your writing productivity or quality, you might generalize and say "I never do anything right" or "I always screw up." By using the words "always" and "never" in this way, you ignore all your talents and success, and create a sense of hopeless failure.

Such simplifications make sense to small children first trying to understand the world. As adults, we grow to appreciate the complexity of life, and can think more clearly about our situations. But when fear takes over, our childhood patterns bubble up and slip past the wisdom we have learned in the intervening decades. Until our top-of-brain regains control, these simplistic thoughts take us along their own illogical track, pulling us further into the fearful state. The resulting state of mind disrupts our creativity and makes it harder to feel hope and courage.

REPLACE GENERALIZATIONS

If you hear yourself using generalizations to bring yourself down, replace them with the nuances and clear thinking you would use in a mature conversation. For example:

Instead of "I never write when I say I'm going to," say the more accurate and uplifting statement, "I often write when I have the opportunity. I enjoy those times. They add up."

Instead of "I always screw up" say "I'm human. I occasionally make mistakes."

Notice that your adult thoughts are less simplistic, and include more detailed observations. Cognitive therapy uses the top of your brain, the story-telling part, to help you rise out of these primitive patterns.

Labels: "I'm lazy."

When used wisely, labels can empower us. For example, in *Your Story as a Writer* section of this book, I talked about using the label "writer" to identify your role in society. In this section you'll see how the power of a label can tear you down.

For example, saying, "I'm lazy" sounds like you are identifying one characteristic of yourself. But such labels are not simply objective assessments. They are loaded with emotional judgments that make it easy to feel bad about yourself and difficult to see how you are going to achieve your goals.

Even though labels describe only one characteristic of a person, we often use them as if they describe the whole person. "I'm lazy" sounds like it pervades every day, and every action, as if laziness is a genetic trait that you can't ever escape or correct.

When they are intended as insults, they can pack a punch. Calling yourself lazy, an idiot, a loser, strips away the positive potential and the many dimensions of being yourself. You awaken the fearful, defensive emotions of your lower brain. By pulling attention away from your top-of-brain, you make yourself feel worthless and small.

REPLACE LABELS THAT UNDERMINE CONFIDENCE

To elevate your thinking to a higher plane, spot unproductive labels that drag you down. When you catch an inner statement like "you idiot," replace the insulting label with uplifting assessments of your situation and character. By focusing on your creative possibilities, you escape the traps imposed by labels.

If you search for a piece of writing buried in a disorganized pile of papers, you might say to yourself, "I'm a slob." This judgment against yourself will stir you to feel bad about yourself, and throw you into bottom-of-brain thinking. Instead, say, "That self-downing accusation is a distraction. I need to focus on my artistic goals."

If you miss a writing session, you might say to yourself, "I'm a bum." That judgment sounds like it ought to prod you to action. But in reality, it makes you feel weak and worthless. Instead make a more nuanced observation about time and energy. "Of course I will miss some writing sessions, but instead of wasting time worrying about it, I could spend two minutes with my notebook, free-writing right now, sketching out a note or two to plan tomorrow's session."

Demoralizing Comparisons

We sometimes assess a situation without noticing that we are actually making a comparison. For example, you might think, "I'm a lousy writer." But hidden within that apparently solid statement you are making a comparison. If you compare yourself with one of your favorite writers, you might reasonably assess yourself as less competent. Or if you think, "writing is difficult" your statement implies a comparison. For example, writing is more difficult than watching television. To manage your emotions more effectively, bring these comparisons out into the open and modify them in order to keep your self-talk upbeat.

REPLACE SELF-DOWNING COMPARISONS

Look under the surface of negative thoughts to find implied comparisons. Playfully explore their false logic and use creativity to substitute more energizing thoughts.

Instead of complaining about who you're worse than, compare yourself to the hundreds of millions of people who don't write at all. Or compare the quality of your writing now with the way you wrote ten years ago. You've come a long way. Or compare yourself with your own future. "I'm a beginner now, compared with the excellent writer I'm going to be in five years."

If you think your project is difficult, imagine how it compares with other activities. Writing is harder than eating an ice cream cone but easier than being a combat soldier. Think of the most miserable thing you've ever done. Then compare your writing with that. On my thirty-first birthday, I stood behind the factory where I was working, helping a plumber clean out the septic system, avoiding splashes of human excrement and feeling sorry for myself. Next to that, any writing project seems like paradise. Stephen Covey teaches another trick. You can give yourself the most energy by thinking, "This is exactly where I want to be right now, because it is taking me in the direction I have chosen to go."

All-or-Nothing: "But if I'm not number one, I quit!"

Anxious, pressured feelings are often triggered by the belief that there are only two possible realities: total success or utter failure, with nothing in between. These two choices work their way into our automatic thinking and provoke feelings of danger and hopelessness.

"If I don't succeed at this task, I've failed forever."

"If it's not perfect, it's awful."

On the surface, these simplistic statements sound logical and compelling. You certainly do want to succeed. And perfection does seem like a worthwhile goal. Because they seem valid, we allow ourselves to dwell on them, entering an almost hypnotic state in which these exaggerated ideas gain credibility. Influenced by their appearance of truth, we feel our emotions sinking, hurtling us into fear, self-defense, and other uncreative states of mind.

Like other unproductive thought patterns, all-or-nothing thinking starts when children first attempt to make sense of the world. When you saw candy, you had to have it immediately or else life was worthless. As you matured, you realized you could add nuances to your thinking. If you don't have it immediately, you might have it later. Or instead of the end of the world, the result of not having it is simply a small, unfulfilled desire. You'll survive.

As you mature from child to adult, you temper all-or-nothing thinking. For example, when you receive a low grade, you recognize it's not the end of the road. It's only a step along a much longer road. A flat tire can be fixed. Heartaches heal. You learn that to maintain emotional balance you must temper your expectations, demands, and extreme thinking. But despite our best efforts, these mature lessons are occasionally brushed aside when, after a rejection letter, a harsh critique, or a missed deadline, your mind careens back into childlike thinking. You can regain your emotional poise by consciously reminding yourself of the lessons you have learned, and willfully apply smart, balanced adult thinking to the mix of thoughts.

REPLACE ALL-OR-NOTHING THINKING

When you reach beyond your comfort zone to new writing goals, not every attempt works out according to plan. When you feel devastated by a rejection or criticism from an editor, or panic because a deadline approaches, catch yourself in the act of all-or-nothing thinking. Replace extreme statements that tear you down with logic that gives you courage. Life is not over. Your writing will continue to improve with practice. Other editors may love it.

Instead of "If I don't succeed like John Grisham or J.K. Rowling, why bother trying?" say, "There are many stages of success, and as my writing grows, I will increasingly satisfy my dreams."

Instead of, "This project isn't perfect," say, "The more I polish this piece, the better it becomes."

To energize yourself, look back across the many steps that brought you this far. Your setbacks were part of the journey, intertwined with learning, determination, courage, and victories. Each success adds up, and over time, you continue to move in the direction of your dreams.

By replacing simplistic thoughts with more nuanced ones, or even with entire stories, your thought process evolves from a childish demand for immediate satisfaction to a mature, adult approach that contains adventure, charm, surprise, and courage.

'Shoulding' Yourself into Submission

Adults use the word "should" to guide small children who are still trying to learn the rules. Unfortunately, the word persists in adult self-talk, where it acquires a harsh, guilt-laden implication. Cognitive therapist Albert Ellis observed that excess, harsh use of the word "should" generates shameful, infantile feelings of failure without offering any insight into the solution.

The inner directive, "I should be writing," can drone on for hours, weeks, and months, making us feel guilty without causing the desired result. On the contrary, the harder we push ourselves with "should" the smaller and more helpless we feel.

"Shoulding" splits us in two. One part feels smug and commanding, the know-it-all parent who says, "Get to your room and study right now." The other part feels like a rebellious child, willing to go to any lengths to defy this voice. The result is a stalemate, an unproductive syndrome that leads to low self-esteem and procrastination.

REPLACE AUTHORITATIVE DEMANDS WITH INSPIRATIONAL ONES

When you hear yourself issuing pressured commands about what you "should" do, replace your statements with more encouraging, collaborative, and kinder ones. What you do today is only one step on a long road. Take your best step, and line yourself up for the next and the next. Consciously focus on your enthusiasm, creative desire, goals, child-like curiosity, and other positive motivations. By using your self-talk to promote patience, persistence, and creativity you will give yourself the best support to achieve your goals.

Instead of "I should be sitting at my desk right now . . . and since I'm not, I'm a bad, lazy person," say "Where I am right now is not helping me achieve my goal. I'll turn off the television, get up, and walk around to break the pattern. Then I'll go to my desk." Or, "Instead of wondering each day when or whether I should be writing, I will develop a daily habit. Writing every day will give me more psychological support to achieve my goals now and in the future."

Becoming Upset About the Future (Crystal-ball Gazing)

A good plan for the future can help us increase the odds of reaching our goals. However, thinking ahead can also result in fear. What if things go wrong? If fear carries us into imagined catastrophes, the resulting worries waste energy without providing anything in return. To energetically move toward your goals, catch yourself in the act of feeling upset about possible failure. Replace these patterns with thoughts that help you focus on your work.

REPLACE WORRY ABOUT THE FUTURE

Prepare for the future by learning skills, improving and producing the pieces you are currently working on, and developing forward momentum based on the successful outcome of your work. If you hear yourself making negative predictions, explain to yourself that you can't actually see the future, and you are wasting time and energy fretting about it. Instead, focus on the effort and creativity of today. "The harder I work today, the better prepared I will be to face tomorrow."

Instead of "This will probably be rejected anyway," say "I am so excited about the possibility of success, that even if I fail this time, I will enjoy the pleasure of anticipation."

Instead of "I will probably give up before I finish," say, "If I keep going, I will continue to experience the joy of striving, and after a while, I will look back and know that these efforts contributed to my self-development."

ADJUST CORE BELIEFS TO BOOST YOUR ENERGY

Cognitive Therapy offers techniques to refute negative thoughts. For example, if you notice yourself thinking, "Everyone will hate my writing," you can edit that thought, and create a more positive statement. Some thoughts vigorously persist, however. If you can't convince yourself to think more positively about some aspect of your writing life, take a closer look at your underlying beliefs. If you really believe it's true, you need to challenge your own assumptions.

Our core beliefs supply the rules upon which we base our lives. We accumulate these rules as we grow up, and they remain under the surface, helping us decide what to think and how to behave. For example, we believe that to get along in society, people should behave courteously and work hard. We apply these beliefs to our own behavior and expect others to do the same. Such beliefs help us interact with people and move toward our goals.

Not all beliefs contribute to our well-being or success. For example, you may believe that optimism is naïve and that pessimism is smarter and more "realistic." Or you may believe that everything you do must be perfect. These are examples of destructive core beliefs. If you believe that pessimism is smart, you will always be looking for bad news, and if you think you are only valid if you are perfect, you will never be valid.

With careful, patient self-development, you can find and redefine beliefs that hold you back. Once you align your beliefs to point toward a harmonious, successful future, walls crumble, giving you access to your creative center.

Strengthen Positive Core Beliefs

Positive beliefs help you sustain your energy. Here are fundamental ones that you can consider. Express them in your own words, to make them yours.

"My writing is valuable to me"

The stimulation and satisfaction that I feel when I write is valuable for my brain, mind, and soul, similar to the value of physical exercise to the body.

"My writing is potentially valuable to others"

My ideas, stories, and information contribute to the world.

"My audience will appreciate my voice"

By striving to reach the readers who are interested in my writing, I become a more active, energized member of society than if I remain silent.

Counteract Unproductive Core Beliefs

Negative core beliefs foster a flurry of irrefutable self-put-downs. For example, if you believe that you are destined to be a mediocre writer, this belief will justify a whole range of self-criticism. Instead of accepting these destructive beliefs, bring them out into the open and consciously unravel them.

"I am a mediocre writer"

Many fine writers fear that exposing their writing will invite ridicule. To succeed, you need to unravel this self-limiting belief. Start by considering the way you were taught to write. In the classroom, you learned that a good grade earns smiles, group praise, and sometimes even gifts and celebrations. Lower grades generate frowns and stern looks, or even worse, a drift toward the anonymous back of the class. For some of us, criticism felt humiliating, especially if we had learning differences, a bullying teacher, or a highly-competitive peer group. Unfortunately, the fears that permeate our childhood psyches are not easy to switch off. For the rest of our lives, when we write, we worry about the repercussions of a "bad grade."

ESCAPE THE GRADING SYSTEM

Replace these potentially humiliating images of a few powerful teachers with the images of hundreds or thousands of readers who will enjoy your work. Readers find pleasure in a variety of ways, such as a good storyline or turn of phrase, a clear idea, or new information. And different readers will appreciate different parts of your work. Their reaction is not unanimous. The nuances of their appreciation covers a broad range of possible reactions. Pleasing readers is a never-ending journey, full of challenges and rewards. It is not a graded test.

Replace Perfectionism

The quest for excellence drives artists forward like adventurers looking for hidden treasure. Excellence is exhilarating, but it is precariously close to its unachievable destructive cousin, perfection. Perfect art is a contradiction in terms, since creativity, by its nature, relies on variations in taste. If you are unconsciously seeking perfection, the quest can weigh you down under rigid, unattainable demands. In its extreme, perfection can make you feel that you are always failing, a demoralizing situation that drains the joy out of your task.

If you believe you must be perfect, then any time you are merely human, you will fall short of your own impossible expectation. To soften your beliefs, consider the importance of variation and "mistakes" in the creative process. When you write whatever comes to mind, without censoring or correcting, you infuse your first drafts with energy. In exchange for letting yourself make mistakes, you connect with your creative source and discover surprising insights and fresh turns of phrase.

To alleviate the pressure to be perfect, explore variations that reduce stress and increase joy. For example, focus on your creative pleasures. "My mind takes flight when I play with words." Or focus on the ambition for creative excellence. "I love writing, and with persistence I will get better and better."

Expose the barrenness of perfectionism by exploring around its edges. For example:

- When editing, be playful. If you see a "flaw" instead of trying to find the "perfect" word, try the silliest, or the most exaggerated. Playfully explore replacing the phrase with the way someone in prison might say the same thing, or the way someone from a different culture might say it. By being playful, you can discover that there is no perfect word, so pick the one that feels most interesting, or quirkiest, or simplest.

- Distorting facts often creates humor. Without such exaggerations and surprising juxtapositions, the world would be less fun. Instead of forcing yourself to look for a perfect word, experiment with exaggerated ones.

- One reason the moon is so appealing to poets is because its roundness comes and goes, and its stains give it unique character.

- Instead of terror at the rigid rules of punctuation, think of commas and dashes as musical notation. Listen to the rhythm of your sentences, and use punctuation to help you find the musicality of your writing voice.

- In life, each moment is filled with variety, unique differences, and new possibilities. Attempt to find this spontaneity in your sentences, too.

WRITING PROMPT

Think of a time when you criticized yourself for being imperfect, such as a particular incident or a typical pattern. Describe the imperfections that seem so awful. Look carefully at these supposed imperfections and talk to yourself about them as if you were encouraging a loved one.

Scan your memory for the earliest time you might have felt this type of frustration with your own behavior. For example, "I'm ten years old, and I turned in a paper with a spelling error. The teacher yelled at me in front of the whole class." Write an imagined or remembered scene of you as a child, and how it felt when someone with so much power criticized you.

Take your abhorrence of "mistakes" to outrageous extremes. For example, write a micro-story about a writer who was fired or arrested for being imperfect.

Exaggerate in the opposite direction. Start from your terrible mistake and write an over-the-top description about a world in which such behavior is considered praiseworthy.

Now, put yourself in the frame of mind of an intelligent, brave adult who understands that every word emanates from your own creative process. Write how you can reframe your attitude toward your writing to allow the creative process to unfold in a more forgiving inner environment, free from fear of imperfection and its consequences.

Rise Above the Impulse to Control

As children, we learn the basic rules of right and wrong. As adults, we judge people based on the degree to which they conform to these expectations. If they break the rules, we call them idiots who didn't act according to the way they "should." Judging other people probably won't change their behavior. A more likely outcome is that when we apply our "shoulds" too rigidly, there is a good chance we will agitate ourselves.

Some of the most exhausting "shoulds" for writers come from the publishing end of our craft. We expect editors and critics to admire our work. And when their responses don't meet our expectations, we criticize them for their lack of good taste. However, these attitudes doom us to dissatisfaction. Since we have no control over their behavior, the more energy we spend judging and chiding them, the less we have available to improve the things we *can* control.

If someone else's behavior outrages, disgusts, or disappoints you, consider how little these emotions accomplish. To counterbalance draining thoughts, substitute more constructive responses such as forgiveness and acceptance. Taking the high road reduces frustration and helps you get where you want to go. Instead of "everyone should behave as I expect" a more effective perspective would be, "I can't control others. I can only control my own effort. If I want to improve the world, I have to start with my own behavior."

Accepting the world as it is has become a centerpiece of the twelve-step programs, which blame many ills on the desire to force the world into conformance to your will. To replace these pressures with poise and peace, repeat the Serenity Prayer:

> God, grant me the serenity to accept the things I cannot change,
> The courage to change the things I can,
> And wisdom to know the difference.

WRITING PROMPT

> Do you get riled up by an editor or a critic who doesn't like your writing? Do you rail against the system that forces you to search so hard for an audience? Write the words that pass through your mind when the world does not bend to your rules. After you list these futile statements, brainstorm productive ones that could create calmness. For example, "I will trust those people who love my work and continue my efforts to please them."

Only Naïve People Are Optimistic

Some people resist visualizing a positive future, believing that optimism is for fools. If you harbor some sort of prejudice against optimism, your belief will hold you back. One approach to changing this belief is to consider how foolish it is. By refusing to see a positive future, you create a prison of hopeless gloom. This demoralizing stance drains energy and makes it more difficult to achieve your goals. Instead of believing that optimism is stupid, flip this belief around and say that only self-destructive people visualize a negative future. They are the ones being foolish.

Since you can't see the future, why make yourself miserable with a negative prediction? Optimism is a powerful technique that gives you more energy and tenacity to achieve a positive outcome. The best approach to the future is to work diligently and creatively today.

"I'm Too Old"

Much of your time is dedicated to survival and responsibility. But the remaining, unstructured time is the canvas on which you paint your creative life. By taking even small steps toward your goals, your progress provides strength and courage to take the next one and the next.

> "Once . . . I had a letter from a nonfiction writer who wanted desperately to write fiction but wondered if sixty was too old to begin. I told her that Elia Kazan was fifty-seven when he started with fiction and that I had published four active octogenarians in a single year. . . . If you're a writer, you not only keep going, but the very act of writing helps

keep you alive."
From *Stein on Writing* by Sol Stein

MORE WORDS TO RISE ABOVE THE BOTTOM-OF-BRAIN

To learn more about the power of positive thoughts, researchers studied a group of people, some of whom suffered from clinical depression. When asked to report on the prevalence of positive thoughts, the group that did not suffer from depression predictably had more positive thoughts than the depressed group. The big surprise came from the fact that both groups had about the same number of negative thoughts.

In other words, the optimists had developed the knack of counterbalancing their negative thoughts with positive ones. You can follow their lead. To maintain a positive attitude conducive to flow, consciously introduce optimistic, wise thoughts about your writing. Use:

- Self-praise

- Affirmations

- Pep talks and other supportive inner conversations

- Quotations from inspiring people

Methods to tilt the scales toward a more positive mood have been touted by optimists throughout the ages. During the twentieth century, superstars like Andrew Carnegie and Norman Vincent Peale became cultural idols, bringing ideas of self-improvement to the masses. Until recently, though, scientifically minded people were skeptical about the effectiveness of such methods, assuming they were rooted in mystical and wishful thinking.

Gradually, evidence accumulated that supported the power of positive thinking. For example, the well-documented "home team" advantage in spectator sports demonstrates that cheering audiences improve their team's performance. Even more obvious is the power of encouragement on children who gain strength from their supportive parents. And for decades, cognitive psychologists have been accumulating evidence that positive thinking affects mood. Finally, in the 21st century, with the advent of brain imaging techniques, we now have scientific evidence that by consciously shifting toward more optimistic thoughts, you can train your neurons to grow accordingly.

Praise Yourself

Many of us feel that praise can be earned only when we finish work, send it out, and receive approval from some impartial reader. Until then, we allow our thoughts to remain critical. By accepting criticism and rejecting praise, we are missing a valuable source of emotional support.

To form a healthier, more energetic relationship with your work, consciously and actively praise yourself for things that you have accomplished, as well for the effort you are putting into achieving your next steps. For every aspect of your writing project you find worthy of praise, say "nice job" or "you are doing so much for your creative dreams."

For example, when you are struggling to achieve some writing goal, don't wait until the end of the product to praise yourself. Celebrate each step. When you invent an interesting plot point for your story, or develop a compelling argument for an essay, give yourself credit. Open your mind to creative ways to praise yourself. Take into account activities that contribute indirectly. For example, praise yourself for honing your skills or for research you will apply toward your writing. This emphasis on achievements provides pleasure and pride.

WRITING PROMPT

Write your praise, telling yourself what a great job you are doing. Put it in a letter or a congratulatory statement. Use genuine, enthusiastic words and don't modify your praise with worries about things you have not done. This is your chance to celebrate the achievements that make you feel good about yourself.

Affirmations: Repeat Phrases that Lift and Inspire

Another way to influence the upbeat quality of your thought stream is to introduce positive phrases, called *affirmations*. Craft your own reaffirming phrases that make you feel good about yourself and your work.

Like other self-talk advice, this at first may sound "artificial." But when you tune into the thoughts running through your mind, you discover you are already repeating things to yourself. Sometimes your automatic thought supports your effort. If you find yourself muttering "I can do that," your self-confident statement boosts your energy. At other times you doubt yourself. If you say to yourself, "I'll never finish," your repetition may undermine your determination. Instead of accepting the automatic thoughts that flow through your mind, craft ones that make you feel better.

Positive pronouncements can realign your energy toward success. You can find such sayings in a variety of places. The twelve-step programs make frequent use of slogans. For example, "One day at a time" helps members achieve sobriety. It also contributes to writing success. Saying it reminds you that each day's progress contributes to the next.

You may prefer the expression "Persistence conquers." It could help you keep going when you falter. Or craft your own saying that makes you feel good about your project.

To build up better thought habits, keep a few affirmations readily available, hanging them on your wall for example or adding them to your calendar. Then repeat them with the same sincerity and intensity as you are accustomed to hearing from your mind's automatic phrases. Let these sayings lift your mood and support your goals.

Internalize Supportive Dialogue

When a child stumbles, a loving parent coos and says, "It's alright. I'm right here." As the child grows older, he or she internalizes this sense of supportiveness and compassion. Similarly, as a writer, there are times when you stumble. If possible, you ask a loved one for a supportive pep talk. Then, by incorporating positive thoughts into your own self-talk, you can internalize such support.

As a writer you have several reasons for imagining internal conversations. Fiction writers imagine conversations all the time. Journalists report on dialogue. And memoir writers attempt to reproduce their verbal exchanges, too. Take advantage of this skill by inserting supportive conversations. Instead of feeling like a victim of your thoughts, insert uplifting support, as if a friend were talking to you, or as if you were speaking as a mentor. To illustrate this process, consider this conversation I had with a friend after she received a sharp criticism of her writing:

"I'm so upset that my work was criticized," she said.

"When you read your piece aloud to a critique group, naturally they offer suggestions," I said.

"Yes, but I wanted them to like it."

"Some probably did like it. Did anyone say anything positive?"

"Yes, I received several compliments, but I keep thinking about the jerk who complained about the lead paragraph."

"If everyone liked it, you wouldn't know what to improve."

"But it hurts."

"That's OK. The twang of pain will pass quickly, and then you're left with valuable information."

> She was quiet for a moment, and then said, "Thanks for that perspective. I can see how criticism points toward some nice improvements. I'm better now."

This woman was seeking a shift in perspective in order to relieve the emotional pressure her thoughts were generating. But if I had not been available, she could have used the incident as a writing prompt, and developed dialogue.

Her emotions had become stuck in a downward direction based on automatic thoughts. By using the art of dialogue writing, you can take the time to work out a more clearly considered perspective, shifting the balance of brainpower from the bottom of your brain, back to the cerebral cortex on top.

Add invented dialogue to your repertoire of techniques for soothing yourself and rising above bottom-of-brain thinking. By exploring verbal interchanges in a creative, problem-solving manner, you will discover a wealth of insights that can help you counterbalance the weight of your original, unproductive thoughts.

As a bonus, by writing such dialogue, you will gain insight into the mental contortions that take place during a conversation between two people, one of whom is riddled with self-doubt and the other who is trying to help. By adding the nuances of self-doubt and internal conflict to characters you are writing in your stories and articles, you will create more realistic, complex situations.

Give Yourself a Pep Talk

When you decide to start a project, you have taken an important step. But you must take a second, equally important action. That is, you must keep going. Both steps, getting started and the determination to keep going, seem simple when you are excited about your project. At other times, you have to coax yourself.

Suppose you are trying to establish the habit of writing for 30 minutes every day. You sit down, turn on your computer, and after five minutes you think, "I don't feel like it." That thought is the enemy. To combat it, perhaps you will glance at a poster on your wall that shows a crowd cheering you to the finish line or you could pull out a stack of index cards and review your affirmations. "You're doing this because you want to." "Rewards wait for those who try."

Sometimes your thoughts and impulses continue to pressure you to quit. What can you do to increase the wisdom, and remain true to your creative longing? Imagine how comforting it would be if you could call upon a wise mentor who gives you the following pep talk:

> "Think about it. You really want to write. You've lined up all your reasons for doing so. You have plans for what you want to write and you anticipate the pleasure of that achievement. Once you get into the flow, you even enjoy it. Once you establish a habit, you will regularly get into the flow. But until then, you have to apply a little *extra* willpower. Look at the next few minutes as the most important minutes of your life. Now focus your attention on your work."

Such a talk would solidify your resolution and help you weather this stormy moment. But what if you don't happen to have a wise mentor standing by? Fortunately, with practice you can learn to talk yourself through these thoughts, and achieve similar goals on your own. Your pep talks will include persuasive reasoning that helps you counterbalance the demands of one part of the mind with the longer vision and higher goals of another part.

Ponder Inspiring Words

Open yourself to advice offered throughout the ages by philosophers, spiritual teachers, poets, and old-timers who have given careful thought to overcoming the negative patterns of mind. Their simple phrases contain profound wisdom that helps us achieve a more effective attitude as we reach for the stars.

You can especially benefit from mentors who speak in the language of positive potential. When inspiring speakers pump you up, open yourself to this influence, and process reality through this lens. Use such thinking to overcome discouragement and other emotional obstacles.

Look in books and on the Internet for advice that resonates with your dreams and provides you with insights to help you make it through difficulties. The authors of these sayings have created them as words to live by. Adding them to your own thoughts confers some of the courageous and energetic thinking for your own use. Here are a few examples:

> "Motivation is food for the brain. You cannot get enough in one sitting. It needs continual and regular refills." - Peter Davies

> "I maintained my edge by always being a student. You will always have something new to learn." - Jackie Joyner-Kersee

> "If you want your life to be a magnificent story, then begin by realizing you are the author and every day you have the opportunity to write a new page." - Mark Houlahan

> "We must all suffer one of two things: The pain of discipline or the pain of regret and disappointment." - Jim Rohn

"Work is love made manifest." - Kahlil Gibran

"People often say that motivation doesn't last. Well, neither does bathing. That's why we recommend it daily." – Zig Ziglar

"To move the world, we must first move ourselves." - Socrates

"Step by step. I can't think of any other way of accomplishing anything." - Michael Jordan

"The victory of success is half won when one gains the habit of setting goals and achieving them. Even the most tedious chore will become endurable as you parade through each day convinced that every task, no matter how menial or boring, brings you closer to achieving your dreams." - Og Mandino

"Sow an act . . . reap a habit; sow a habit . . . reap a character; sow a character . . . reap a destiny." - George D. Boardman

"I never could have done what I have done without the habits of punctuality, order, and diligence, without the determination to concentrate myself on one subject at a time. . ." - Charles Dickens

"We gain strength, and courage, and confidence by each experience in which we really stop to look fear in the face . . . we must do that which we think we cannot." - Eleanor Roosevelt

 "The limits of the possible can only be defined by going beyond them into the impossible." - Arthur C. Clarke

"It is a paradoxical but profoundly true and important principle of life that the most likely way to reach a goal is to be aiming not at that goal itself but at some more ambitious goal beyond it." - Arnold Toynbee

"I wasn't going to be one of those people who died wondering 'what if?' I would keep putting my dreams to the test–even though it meant living with uncertainty and fear of failure. This is the shadowland of hope, and anyone with a dream must learn to live there." – Alex Haley

"When one door of happiness closes, another opens, but often we look so long at the closed door that we do not see the one that has been opened for us." – Helen Keller

"The ancient Greek definition of happiness was the full use of your powers along lines of excellence." - John F. Kennedy

You might also have heard quotable quotes from the people in your life. My grandmother used to say, "This, too, shall pass." When I was a child I didn't know what she was talking about. As I've grown older, I understand the wisdom and strength conveyed by these simple words, and now when I repeat this expression, I feel her strength and support.

My favorite saying is the one that is engraved on my older brother's tombstone, "*Ad astra, per aspera*" a Latin expression that means, "To the stars through difficulty." The expression inspires me. I imagine the difficulties Ed must have overcome to become a medical doctor and start a family. When I see it on his grave, I wonder if his epitaph points beyond those successes, toward the real stars. The saying calls to me to aim toward sublime goals, and ignore hardships along the way.

POSITIVE SELF-TALK THROUGHOUT YOUR JOURNEY

Inner dialogue plays a role at every step along a writer's path. For example, if you hate research, your silent complaining could add difficulty to the process. Likewise, to write your first draft, you must quiet your analytical thinking while you record your first thoughts. When you shape, edit, and polish your work, self-talk helps you stay the course. And positive self-talk helps you build skills, receive critiques, send out queries, and handle rejection.

So when you are struggling with any aspect of your writing goal, consider what you are saying to yourself about the task. Then, modify these statements so your self-talk energizes you and helps you overcome the problem

WRITING PROMPT

To become more conscious of positive self-talk, try to catch yourself thinking excited, creative, optimistic thoughts while free-writing, editing, organizing, or querying. Take a moment to write these in a journal. Then, when you need an infusion of good energy, review this journal to remind yourself of motivational statements that arise from your own mind.

Consider moments along your writing journey when you feel drained or intimidated. What statements exaggerate the project's difficulty, importance, or urgency? To improve your feelings, review this journal and next to each negative statement, write the counterbalancing positive statements that restore your mood.

Note: When you attempt to reach out to readers, your thoughts about their reactions become especially important. I'll focus on improving this aspect of your internal dialogue in the Love Like a Writer *section.*

Plan to Insert Positive Thoughts When You Need Them

When negative thoughts bubble up from your unconscious they seem so "real," you believe they are true. Instead of waiting for these thoughts to sweep you into their hypnotic spell, enlist the planning part of your brain. Develop a plan to insert positive sayings to strengthen your resolve, weather the storm of negative thoughts, and return safely to the energetic pursuit of your goals. For example,

- Write them on 3" x 5" index cards.

- Print them in large letters and frame them.

- Stick notes on the wall.
- Put them on your screen saver.
- Memorize them.

WRITING PROMPT

Write a plan to:

Find and create positive statements.

Record them.

Carry or post reminders to make them readily accessible.

Insert them into your thought process when you need them.

Using your awareness of self-talk and self-limiting beliefs, review some of the objections that block your progress. Select positive, constructive word choices that boost your energy. Avoid complaints and self-criticism. When you feel yourself in an unproductive mood, explore the relationship between what you say and how you feel, and then select more energized phrases.

Complete the following sentences:

What do I say to myself when I'm feeling blocked or "wasting" time, or incompetent, unloved, or afraid of failure . . .?

If someone said this to me, I would feel . . .

A statement that makes me feel better is . . .

Love Like a Writer

WRITERS COMMUNICATE WITH READERS

To gain deeper insight into becoming a writer, consider the first words a baby speaks. Imagine a tiny person pointing at a ball. She hesitates, furrows her brow, and then utters the syllable, "ball." She peers up into her father's eyes. A smile crosses his lips. He reaches down to hug her, cooing, "That's right, Precious. It's a *ball*." One uttered word magically opens the floodgates of love.

As we learn about language, our words grow more complex, and at every step they connect us with each other. We express our needs through words and expect a response when we talk to others. Our parents coach us, and we try to please them. Soon we notice the effect of spoken words. Speech carries us from infancy to a wider social world.

When we're ready, we advance to writing. Our first exposure seems technical, Our teachers think it's important, but we have not yet grasped the value. Then one day, we discover that writing can evoke emotion.

During my first month-long stay at summer camp, huddled on a bunk with paper and pen, we write home, attempting to share our day. Written words reveal a new potential. They can carry thoughts and feelings across distance.

Back at school the following autumn, instead of using words to express love, we learn more grammar, and then focus on literature. We learn the power of the written word through the ages. The Greek epics of *The Iliad* and *The Odyssey* still move us, thousands of years after they were written. The novels and poetry of the nineteenth and twentieth centuries connect us with men and women in different parts of the world and in situations outside our experience. Movie scripts move us to laughter, tears, and inspiration.

You know that words connect you with people, and in a moment of loneliness, or creative ambition, or a desire to share some image or idea, you wonder if you, too, might affect strangers with your words. But you've never learned how to use words to move hearts and minds, so you must develop the habit.

You write a story about your teenage years, when your dad loaned you his car for a high school date and you ran a red light. Your initial draft flows easily. You remember your heart pounding, trying to think of what to say to your date. Should we hold hands? You were jolted out of your thoughts by a crash that sent the car spinning. *What happened? One moment I was on a date. The next, in a wrecked car.* You sat there in a daze. Then the cops came, and neither of you was really hurt, and then somewhere in there was a humiliating call to your dad.

You look at what you've written. As writing teacher Sol Stein says, first-draft words come from the top of your head. They have no power or pizzazz.

You're not even sure how stories are supposed to work. How do you introduce the event? What's the point? It just hangs there as a humiliating episode in a generally awkward time in your life. You take a class and try it again. You realize that you are attempting to convey something to a reader. But what? You fill in more background. Add details. Search for a clever or meaningful end.

You struggle with the requirements of writing. You can't just end the story by laughing or looking embarrassed. Readers cannot see your face or hear your intonations. Nor can they ask questions. When you write it, you must be clear and complete and also inject enthusiasm and wit into your sentences. But in these early efforts, showing emotions through the written word feels as clumsy as trying to tie your shoes while wearing mittens. You keep trying, revising this piece more times than you expected.

When you think you're done, you send it to a critique group. They give you feedback, and you edit it further. You want a stranger to feel the things you felt. Finally, you achieve the quality you aimed for, and someone you respect says "Good story." You feel a surge of creative relief and pride, equivalent to what happened to that little girl who said "ball." You have been trying to transmit what's inside your mind to someone else, and you succeeded.

Some Writing Stays Private

Some writing, such as diary entries or brainstorming notes, are intended only for yourself. Creating such reader-less writing serves you in many ways. It bolsters you when you're feeling down, provides a fresh perspective, reminds you of lessons you already know, and creates images that entertain you. People who write for themselves report a sense of euphoria, of completion, contentment, and satisfaction when they wrap interesting words around their emotions.

Reach Out to Micro-audiences

When we write an email to a friend, our reader knows who we are and why we are writing. Even if we make a clumsy statement, we can recover with the help of follow-up questions and explanations. And because of our preexisting relationship, we don't have to convince our friend to read the letter.

Even though informal writing requires less discipline than writing for strangers, it requires considerably more skill than merely writing for ourselves. In a letter or email, we must clearly say what we mean in a manner that someone else will understand. And with this additional effort comes social rewards. Consider some examples offered by workshop attendees:

"I've always enjoyed writing letters to my cousins. After I retired, this became an extremely valuable connection even though we hadn't seen each other for years."

"When my mother died, there was a lot I wanted to say in her memory, but I couldn't imagine speaking at the funeral. 'No way. I'm no public speaker.' Then, I wrote my thoughts, and read my prepared statement. Sharing my thoughts publicly helped me bring closure to our relationship, and I believe it helped her friends as well."

"I've always loved to write, so when my kids started school, I decided to start a little newsletter to share their milestones with our extended family."

WRITING PROMPT

> Scan your memory for situations when writing connected you with people. What sort of bond did it create? What sort of satisfaction did you feel? Recall a moment when your writing inspired an emotional release or opened a door with another individual. Or write about the time when you wished you could have had this effect.

Write for Work

Combine your desire to write with your need to earn a living by working as a journalist, technical writer, or marketer. You may not be fulfilling every aspect of the writing life, but you will be gaining valuable experience while developing confidence.

A student in a workshop said, "When the people at work realized I can write, they asked me to summarize the departmental meeting. This turned out to be a great stepping stone for my career, and it was fun getting paid to write."

Write in Forms Strangers Want to Read

To reach a broader audience, your writing must appeal to readers who will only know you through your words. The writing must speak for itself. They can't see your face and can't ask you questions. An even more daunting requirement of writing for strangers is that you must convince them to read your particular piece out of the million options available.

To gain a clearer understanding of how to achieve these goals, review the material you enjoy reading. By the time you have selected a piece to read, you have unconsciously gone through dozens of micro-decisions. Are you interested in the subject, the type of writing, the mood conveyed by the title and cover?

When you become a writer, you must learn to fulfill these expectations for your readers. Reverse the process you used to select a book and instead decide what you could write that might appeal to someone else. Perhaps the most fundamental decision is the form of the writing. What sort of medium will speak to your readers?

NONFICTION ESSAYS AND ARTICLES

Essays are based on your opinions and experience. A good essay presents thoughts in a clear, compelling sequence. Articles consist of facts, interviews, and anecdotes arranged into readable prose. A good article includes intriguing, valuable information, organized to inform readers. Sometimes, essays and articles combine, using research and information to convey the author's compelling message.

WRITING PROMPT

> List some of the topics you want to cover in an essay or article. Who would read these pieces? Gather a list of online and print publications that might publish them. Focus on a few and hone your style to match theirs.

NONFICTION BOOKS

A nonfiction book explores a subject in great depth, so it takes longer to write than an article–a lot longer. And the economics of publishing a book are completely different from publishing article, requiring a search for an agent, and then a lengthy proposal and pitch process. And once a book gets published, you need to put your own energy into marketing and selling your book.

While the challenges are great, the potential rewards are great, as well. For one thing, books are the backbone of civilization. If you write a book that has lasting power, it could influence and entertain people for years. And by writing a nonfiction book, you will become so knowledgeable about your topic that you may become known as an expert, sought out for information on your subject.

> "I was talking about vampires one night with some friends and was shocked at how much folklore they had wrong. I told them if that's all they knew about vampires, they would be defenseless against attacks. From the discussion, I got the idea to write my book about vampire folklore through history. After the book was published, I was invited to speak at anthropology conferences. There I was with my degree in journalism and a book about folklore lecturing to a room full of scholars."
> Jonathan Maberry, bestselling thriller writer and vampire expert

WRITING PROMPT

Do you want to write a book-length work or shorter pieces? Fiction or nonfiction? If fiction, are you writing mystery, romance, or literary? If nonfiction, is it self-help, memoir, or how-to? What specific topic? Who will read your writing? Veterans? Teenagers? Retirees? What would you offer them? Entertainment? Information? Inspiration?

Visit a bookstore or library and review books similar to the one you want to write. Summarize in a few paragraphs how yours compares with each one that has already been published. Profile a likely reader for your own book idea, and a likely reader for each of the books you found on the shelf.

NOVEL, SHORT STORY, MOVIE SCRIPT, PLAY

To write a compelling story, you must learn the various subcomponents of that skill, such as character, plot, pacing, and dialogue. During your initial attempts, it is too early to ask if your story meets the readers' needs to be entertained. Instead ask for feedback from fellow writers who can help you improve your skills.

The first time you publish a story for strangers, you move from the flatlands of a consumer into the foothills of a creator. Like a hero, you keep going. By striving to reach bestselling lists, you expand your horizons, offering readers gifts such as entertainment, insight, and connection.

WRITING PROMPT

What experience have you had creating fictitious characters, worlds, and situations? Describe how you feel when you write about events that have, until that moment, existed only in your own mind.

CREATIVE NONFICTION AND MEMOIR

Creative nonfiction is a fascinating form of writing that exists at the crossroads of nonfiction and story. By learning to find stories in real life, you can create compelling accounts based on facts, characters, and events. You could perform this creative feat for the situations in your town, for example, by following a person and seeing how they overcome obstacles and achieve goals.

In a memoir, you could tell the story of your own experience. By using your own life as a creative work, you can offer a variety of nonfiction benefits to your readers – for example, enhancing information through your particular perspective. And by applying the structure of story, you offer suspense and entertainment.

WRITING PROMPT

> Do you tell stories at family gatherings or children's groups? How do you feel when you your audience laughs or sighs? What value are you giving them when you tell the story? What do you get in return?

POETRY

The poet spends time caressing each word, and assumes the reader will do the same. This requires a different pace than prose. Driving down the long road of life, hurtling toward the horizon, poets pull off to the shoulder, get out of the car, kneel, and gaze longingly at a purple wildflower as if they had never seen a flower before. Words at this level of intensity may inspire an almost mystical falling in toward implications, contrasts, rhythms, and rhymes. Poetry creates an intimate connection, joining writer and reader in an introspective embrace. Many poets experience writing as a part of their search for meaning, and lovers of the genre band together in a subculture with its own groups, websites, journals, and e-zines.

WRITING PROMPT

> Pretend you could overcome all commercial obstacles and share your poetry with others. Describe how that would feel. What do you hope to give your readers? What do you hope to get in return?

Readers Turn Writing into a Social Act

Whatever form you choose, you must continue to improve your craft and develop a relationship with readers. This is the road the writer travels. Through your written words, you offer yourself to your culture. We all rely on your contribution. Your words link us, guide us, entertain us, and connect the knowledge upon which we build our worlds.

OUT OF PRIVACY AND INTO THE PUBLIC

In the play *My Fair Lady*, Eliza Doolittle's lower-class birth dooms her to remain poor for the rest of her life. A linguistic expert helps Eliza escape that destiny simply by providing her with better command of the language. Even though the British class system has changed dramatically over the last hundred years, the play makes an important observation that resonates today: Our use of language influences the way people perceive us. This feature of social interaction applies not only to proper accents. Good writing also has the power to connect us with strangers. When we learn how to communicate with them, we can expand beyond our own small circle.

This transition, from being unnoticed by strangers to being appreciated by them, requires more than just literary skills. It also requires emotional ones. To succeed, we must push through a variety of emotions. Certainly, not every reader will be impressed by our work. Some might even be offended by it. If an editor isn't wild about our writing, or a reviewer pans it, we must keep our self-esteem intact. Supported by positive emotions and undeterred by bad ones, we write and submit again and again, practicing, learning, and growing.

Your Inner Supporters Encourage You at Every Step

You may hope to succeed without any concern for your audience. Once you're famous, they'll love you and everything will be fine. To reach that point, however, you need energy and inspiration now. To hasten your growth as a writer, instead of waiting for your audience to materialize, try to tap into their expectations. As you write, imagine them eagerly listening.

You can't know the individual tastes of your future readers, and yet, somehow you must arrange your words to influence their thoughts and feelings. How is that possible? The best suggestion I've heard is to write the way you would talk to a good friend. I love that image. I can think back in my life to fabulous discussions that lasted for hours, trying to find the meaning of life. But when I attempted to base my writing on that model, I couldn't imagine a friend with such varied and sustained curiosity.

On the contrary, the audience that kept popping into my mind was a judgmental, harsh, and sometimes angry crowd. No matter how hard I tried to avoid the image, I saw myself on a stage, as if at an inquisition; someone in the audience shouted, "Why did you say that?" and the others grumbled accusingly in the background. Rather than write to this belligerent mob, I shut down the whole image and returned to the isolation of the readerless writer.

In tiny steps, I continued to search for real readers. I published a newspaper column. I swapped pieces with my critique group. I posted articles on my website. Time after time, I received feedback from kind, curious people. These supportive images gradually populated my imagination, crowding out the edgy ones that formerly scared me.

The biggest shift in my attitude toward readers came after I started teaching classes and speaking at writing groups. I looked out at the smiling, curious faces and someone asked a question. My mind became engaged. Clear, compelling sentences sprang to mind, complete with examples that illustrated my points. After experiencing real people, my dark fantasies faded, replaced by kind, energizing listeners. Even when I'm alone, I can conjure these images, generating the kind of verbal flow that writing teachers recommend.

By writing toward imagined friends and readers, I was able to increase the energy and quality of my writing. Ultimately, by trusting my readers, I earned their trust. When they enjoyed my writing, they recommended it to friends, transforming my relationship with readers from fantasy to reality.

WRITING PROMPT

To whom do you wish you could communicate your story or information? Take your time and scan through your experiences. What person or group would energize you, perhaps because of their curiosity and openness, or their need for this information? Free-write an event or idea as if you are talking to this friendly audience.

To work toward a friendly, supportive group, try to clarify some of their characteristics. By bringing them into focus, you can change your visualization from an abstract, faceless crowd, to a more specific group.

When you publish your work, who will read it? How old are they? Where were they born? Are you addressing all English-speaking girls or boys between the ages of 10 and 12? Mothers who grew up in single-parent families? Forty-year-old working men who grew up reading science fiction? How much education do they have? What makes them tick? What are they curious about? What do they do with their day?

By writing for specific readers, you are entering into a relationship with them. You are working hard to give them the most readable, enjoyable, or informative message. In turn, they are giving you their attention, time, and sometimes, money. If you feel a warm glow of admiration for them, and a comfortable sense of kinship, your thoughts and attention will flow toward them.

If your early attempts to visualize an audience feel uncomfortable, back away, and try another strategy. In one playful imagined scene, I befriended my inner critic, and asked her to turn her critical intensity toward the rest of the audience. She stood watch over their reaction, and ensured that only those who were attentive and enjoyed my work were permitted to stay.

WRITING PROMPT

> What do you like about your audience? What would you feel,
> meeting and socializing with these people? Who in your life do
> they remind you of? Are they like your kids, parents, teachers,
> neighbors, schoolmates, clients? What do you want to give them?
> How do you wish to affect their lives? How will they feel during
> and after reading your work? Will their lives be different?

Writing to a supportive imagined audience became an important step in my writing life, enabling me to visualize the effect my words might have on readers. These imagined people have taken the time to read my words. My desire to please them provides intensity and focus. I want to give them the best experience I possibly can.

Prepare for Real Readers with Small Informal Audiences

To learn how to write for readers, ask other writers for feedback. Their responses help us learn what our words sound like to someone else. Drink in explicit or implied praise to gain an emotional boost and reinforce appreciation for what you are doing right. Listen for information that can help you improve. By "writing out loud," we are breaking the silence, moving beyond just writing for ourselves.

Naturally, we feel anxious about their responses. What if we have been deluding ourselves? What if they hate it? Some actually might hate your work, and that is part of the learning process. Like a child playing in a schoolyard, look at the bruises as part of the game. Accepting that you can't please everyone will free you from perfectionism and help you concentrate on pleasing those who enjoy your work.

Another way to promote your awareness of an audience is to start posting on a blog. Even if you only have one reader, you will begin to experience the trepidation and exhilaration of communicating with a stranger. And with persistence, your writing will improve, you will sharpen your offerings, and your audience will grow.

Eye Contact with Your Audience

When I completed my graduate degree in Counseling Psychology, under the supervision of a seasoned professional, I attempted to go into private practice. I expected that the modest sign I put out on the busy road in front of the office would attract more clients than I could handle. After a few months, I wondered why I was still alone. Where were the throngs?

I turned to my supervisor to help me make sense of what was happening and how to proceed. He told me that since clients were not finding me, I needed to find them. To do so, I should speak in front of groups. His suggestion felt like a cruel taunt. Like the joke by comedian Jerry Seinfeld, I was deathly afraid of speaking in public. Seinfeld quipped, "According to most studies, people's number one fear is public speaking. Number two is death. Death is number two. Does that seem right? That means to the average person, if you have to go to a funeral, you're better off in the casket than doing the eulogy."I laughed at the joke, but hated the reality.

I did, however, love to write. I joined a writing group and improved my skills. I had no problem writing alone in my room. When I tried to reach readers, I ran into the same challenge with writing as I had with public speaking. I avoided submitting to larger publications because of my fear of rejection.

Eventually, I recognized that the scarcity of clients at my therapy practice, my unwillingness to speak to groups, and my reluctance to pitch my writing were all symptoms of the same inner conflict. I was asking strangers to trust me, and yet I was unwilling to trust them.

To change, I forced myself to attend a meeting of Toastmasters International, a nonprofit organization that helps people open up in front of groups. At the coffee break, I nervously asked a gray-haired gentleman if it was possible for a profoundly shy person to learn to speak with confidence. He assured me that when he started, he, too, experienced terror. He said "Toastmasters is magic."

Despite the healthy, friendly environment of the group, my internal pressure was overwhelming. At my first attempt to give a talk at Toastmasters, I stammered. I felt humiliated and helpless, and after a few meetings, I quit.

Recognizing that I must overcome this problem, I turned to my self-help books, and reviewed everything I knew about coping with anxiety. *Breathe deeply. Talk yourself through it. Start slowly.* I even learned a few new techniques. *Carry flash cards and just before you start, remind yourself of all the reasons you want to do this.*

A year later, I returned to Toastmasters and this time I stayed, forcing myself to complete the exercises in their program. By the end of that series, my anxiety had diminished to the extent that I began looking for opportunities to speak to other groups.

When I started teaching workshops about the psychology of writing, I could look at my audience in person. Their presence added a new, important dimension to my understanding of how to communicate to strangers. In addition to the positive feedback I felt from people who seemed attentive, I also learned valuable lessons from those who looked away. In my early talks, I assumed if they weren't looking at me, they were displeased or bored. I tried to ignore them, focusing instead on those who were smiling and nodding. After the talks were over though, the ones who seemed to be lost in thought were often the ones who came up to thank me personally. They were taking it all in and thinking about it. Just like readers! Their extra effort to express their appreciation finally convinced me that I had been judging my audiences far more harshly than they had been judging me.

My public speaking helped me in surprising ways. To prepare for public appearances, I gave practice talks in my basement to an empty room, while I walked on the treadmill. Once I became comfortable with this technique, I realized it could help me with my writing. When I was stuck writing a difficult passage, I got back on the treadmill and tried to explain my idea to the empty room. By this time, my imagined crowd of angry listeners had been replaced by kind, curious listeners like the people I met at Toastmasters and at my writing groups. By talking about my idea aloud, the flow of words helped me return to my keyboard with greater clarity.

After I published the first version of this book, I discovered that the combination of writing and public speaking connected me more with my readers than either activity did alone. When I was invited to my first interview on public radio, I couldn't believe how cool it was to know my voice could be heard throughout the region. Conquering my fears of trying to reach the public had been a key step on my journey to become a writer.

MORE WAYS TO CONNECT WITH YOUR AUDIENCE

Shift Your State of Mind and Become an Audience Member

In my forties, I read Joan Baez's memoir *And a Voice to Sing With*, in which she said that the most tragic thing she could imagine, would be for someone to die without knowing the pleasure of singing. I didn't want to fall into that sad state so I decided to accept the challenge. I took private lessons to learn the basics. Then, to experience singing in the company of others, I joined a choir. At first, I was so intent on hitting the right notes that I paid no attention to the other voices. After a few years, something remarkable happened. I began to listen. The ability to hear my voice blending with theirs helped me adjust tone, volume, and rhythm.

Emboldened by my discovery that I could express myself in new forms, in my fifties I decided to seek the pleasure of writing for an audience. Until then, my only writing had been in my journal or for readers of technical manuals. I had never developed a writer's voice, and had no idea if it was even possible. I read books on the subject and attended workshops and gradually acquired skills. But my biggest problem was that I didn't know how my words would sound to others. Over time, I discovered methods that allowed me to "hear" my own writing.

To listen to my own written words, I needed to create a little distance between the act of writing and the act of reading. To create a different state of mind, I experimented with various techniques and found ones that worked most effectively for me. Each technique contributed to my ability to "hear" myself, providing me with the feedback I needed to keep improving.

You have been a reader for many years. You know what you like. You know what rings true. Take advantage of your own expertise by becoming a reader of your writing. The methods are simple, and yet contribute valuable feedback to help you write material worth reading.

READ DURING DIFFERENT PARTS OF THE DAY

At different times of the day, you experience varying degrees of relaxation, fatigue, alertness, distractions, and so on. So to hear your writing in a different state than when you wrote it, develop the habit of writing in the morning and reading your work in the afternoon, or the other way around.

READ IN A DIFFERENT ENVIRONMENT

Similarly, your environment changes your state of mind. For example, write in the coffee shop and read at your desk, or do it the other way around. Read it while relaxing in an easy chair. Turn on music when reading, and vary the type of music. One of my most effective methods is to take a printed copy with me on the treadmill and mark it up while I'm walking.

USE YOUR EARS

Read it aloud, or ask someone to read it to you, or record it and listen to the recording while you are out for a walk.

GIVE IT TIME

Set it aside and come back to it in a few hours or days. By allowing some time to pass between the act of writing and the act of reading, you can "hear" your writing from a different vantage point.

The challenges I faced when trying to hear my own writing "voice" turned out to be remarkably similar to the progress I had made in singing. Once I learned to "hear" my own writing, I was able to adjust and tune it to the sound I was trying to achieve.

To experience your own work the way others will perceive it, put yourself into a reading frame of mind. Relax and experience the flow of words. Note your own response. If a phrase causes you to stumble, it will probably create the same reaction in other readers. And if you feel goose bumps or your eyes tear up, it's a sign that your writing has hit its mark.

Friendships and Meetings with Other Writers

The best way to learn what your writing sounds like to readers is to ask them. In critique groups, readers will give you insight into your writing that you would not have considered, no matter how many times you read it yourself. Some of them will point out what you've done right. Some will provide tips about how to improve. And all of the feedback helps you grasp the complexity and creative challenge of trying to "speak" to strangers.

The group environment, in addition to giving you feedback, overcomes the isolation of being a writer. Your companions understand what you're going through. They share your aspirations and offer each other tips about publishing and networking opportunities.

Every group has its own personality. If one group doesn't satisfy you, try another one. Explore your local library, college, community center, the Internet, or start your own group.

Free-writing Together

Some groups offer you the chance to write during meetings. As you see others let go and think spontaneously, you get permission to do the same. The scratching of their pens harmonizing with your own provides an immediate sensory experience of writing together. And intense focus of timed writing can stimulate your creativity so effectively, you forget all about your inner critic.

In the meeting, you will all respond to a writing prompt offered by the leader. Or you might get the prompts from a book, or by asking each member to bring in a suggestion and then voting on them, or picking one at random. Or you could develop some other technique for liberating your writing voice from its routine. For example, here is an innovative approach from the book *Writing Together: How to Transform your Writing in a Writing Group* by Dawn Denham Haines, Susan Newcomer, and Jacqueline Raphael:

WRITING PROMPT

> Label four envelopes with the words: person, place, object, and situation. You can adapt this to fiction, using more imaginative elements, or to memoir by using places and characters from everyday life. Then each person in the group writes a story element on a slip of paper and places it in the appropriate envelope. To start the writing exercise, randomly select one story element from each envelope, and then for ten or twenty minutes, everyone writes a micro-story.

Since the components of the story are chosen independently, they force you to create surprising connections and liberate you from your left-brain plans. Sharing these surprises in a group is an empowering experience. After experimenting with writing prompts, you can learn techniques to stimulate your own free-writing sessions.

Train Your Mind to Absorb Praise

When someone praises your work, do you dismiss the compliment with an automatic, "He's not very smart"? Or do you doubt his motives? Even if you don't outright reject compliments, perhaps you let them slip by unnoticed. You can improve your relationship with your readers, and gain a source of emotional support, by taking a deeper drink from the well of praise.

To explore your attitude about this simple gesture of appreciation, switch roles for a moment and consider your reaction to a book that you have recently read. Notice the complexity of your thoughts about it. The story may have evoked scenes or situations that gave you pleasure. It might have surprised you with insights or psychological twists. You might have enjoyed turns of phrase, humor, or clever dialogue. In addition, many of your reactions to the book may have related to memories in your own life or associations with other writing you have recently read.

Now, keeping in mind your multidimensional reaction to another author's work, imagine someone saying to you, "I like your book." Take a moment to consider all the nuances of their thoughts and feelings while reading the book. The longer you dwell there, the more complicated your analysis becomes.

Then, back away from this maze. Instead of analyzing what you can't see, take a closer look at the emotional implications of their praise. Open yourself to the kindness and the generosity implied by the gesture. They read your book, felt your intention, received whatever they could from you, and chose to send you back a simple statement of support. "Thanks for all you do for your readers."

Allow this moment to soothe your desire to be appreciated and validated. Find a place within yourself that is worthy of your audience's love, and let their appreciation flow to that place. Your warm regard for them turns them into friends, and fills you with enthusiastic energy.

When someone praises you in person, quiet your mind and drink in their words and body language. If you catch yourself thinking along lines that diminish the value of the praise, tell yourself firmly that these thoughts are not appropriate. To help you absorb the statement, repeat it aloud. When someone says, "I really like your piece" say, "I'm glad you really like it." Look them in the eye, think about what they are saying, and thank them for the compliment.

Enjoy praise with at least as much ferocity as you dislike criticism. Become so attuned to praise that if out of a hundred people, one person praises you, you feel successful. By becoming hyper-aware of this moment, you will absorb it completely, and then have it available as a memory to absorb again later. This encouragement, as simple as a phrase and a smile, is your compass, your bull's eye, your holy grail. These are the people for whom you are writing. Let them cheer you on.

Focus on Your Service

Of course you want people to like what you write, but no matter how hard you seek admiration, you can never precisely measure it. Like a sand dune, your audience's reaction changes shape and size with the wind. They like some parts better than others. They may be inspired by your message, yet unimpressed by your word choices, or the other way around. They may like one page better than the next. Even famous authors win acclaim for one work and not for another. Your audience's response belongs to them, not you, and it is impossible to manage it or even know it.

Since you can't control or measure their response, focus on what you can control. Ask yourself what you are attempting to provide. Entertainment? Information? Inspiration? Whatever you are attempting to give them, give more. By doing your best to provide these services, you will increase your audience's enjoyment and win their admiration.

When you find yourself worrying about their responses, bring your mind back to improving your product. Every time you revise a paragraph, take a class, or send your work for a critique, concentrate on increasing the quality of your service.

WRITING PROMPT

Instead of telling yourself "They might not like it," ask "What steps can I take this week to do my job better?" or "What steps can I take this year to do my job better?"

To reinforce your focus on effort, say, "To improve my relationship with my audience, today I will admire them, love them, trust them, serve them, even more than I already do."

Experiment, Explore, and Combine

You work hard to develop compelling, well-crafted sentences. Excellent writing is only the first half of your mission, though. To complete your task, these sentences must enter the minds of your readers. Inject your writing with fresh, lively energy by visualizing your communication with curious, perceptive readers. Instead of waiting for those curious readers to come calling, make an effort to reach out to them. Here are a few activities that can help you get in touch with this aspect of your writing:

- Explain your subject in a letter to a friend.

- Deliver a talk or tell a story to a live audience.

- Teach in a classroom or workshop. Preparing for the talk will enrich your energy and vocabulary. This is a great way to become engaged in a topic, as well as to break down the barriers between yourself and an audience.

- Write a biographical sketch of your "ideal" reader.

- Discuss or interview people to learn what they think about your subject. Their ideas may evoke insights that can improve your piece.

- Role-play your characters in front of an imaginary, appreciative audience.

- Chat with an editor or a successful writer and learn more about their relationship to readers.

- Decorate your desk with photographs of an audience listening attentively or cheering wildly.

- Attend writer's conferences, workshops, and classes. While you are soaking up insights into your writing, soak up the presence of other writers, with their own hopes, dreams, and fears.

- Share peer critiques in a writing group or online support network.

WRITING PROMPT

Write about how you will put one or more of these suggestions in place. Instead of writing a plan, try writing a scene. For example, put yourself at the front of the room, energizing your audience with your story. Or write a scene in which one of your readers calls a friend to describe why your book is worth reading. By using your own imagination, or remembering situations in which you felt warm regard, you can enhance your relationship with your readers and allow them into your life.

Bonus: Advanced Audacity

COURAGE TO SEEK READERS AND GATEKEEPERS

Until recently, the responsibility for producing and selling books fell on the publishing company, whose staff designed the cover, wrote the blurb, and sold it to bookstores. Today, self-published and traditionally published authors must convince strangers to buy our works. If you feel intimidated by your future readers or by the editors, agents, and reviewers who provide access, you will hold back. And if you distrust them, you will have a hard time convincing them to trust you.

Many writers want to stay safely at their writing desks, avoiding the public altogether. By following their preference for privacy, however, they severely limit their connection with readers. If you are an introvert and have spent a lifetime cultivating your relationship with your own mind, you are in company with many aspiring writers who prefer working in private.

According to Susan Cain, author of *The Power of Introverts in a World That Can't Stop Talking*, introversion and extroversion are measurable qualities that describe a person's personality. For most of us, one of these tendencies will be far more comfortable than the other. To succeed, we must master the psychological skills required for going in the uncomfortable direction. That's where courage comes in. Hero-writers face the long journey with courage, and when the going gets too rough, heroes ask for help and study new techniques.

Your fears will fade once you have demonstrated to yourself that standing in front of a roomful of people won't kill you, and rejection from an agent won't ruin you. To learn these lessons for yourself, apply techniques to help you over the initial hurdles. In the following sections, I explore the causes of social anxiety, and some effective methods to help reduce its impact. As you progress up the mountain toward ever-greater challenges, you may need to call on these techniques again and again.

Why Should We Fear Readers?

It seems irrational to feel intimidated by potential readers who don't exist yet. Despite the illogic of your reaction, the fear seems real, creating heart palpitations, sweaty palms and weak knees. To avoid these feelings, you turn your mind away from your own goals, planning your escape. Why react to these social dangers as if they were violent attacks?

All animals obey powerful survival instincts – wired deep into their brains – that stir up emergency action in order to save themselves from danger. These mechanisms of fear instantly cause our hearts to race if we, say, see an object hurtling toward us on the highway. Humans are social animals, however, and if we offend someone, or worse, offend everyone, we can trigger a response as dangerous to our brains as if we were being attacked by lions.

Conventions that restrict acting out in public protect us from social chaos, and so we prefer to obey them. But for writers who want to break out of privacy, our attempts to reach agents or readers can arouse similar concerns. If we unconsciously believe that searching for readers might endanger our position in the community, we will feel intimidated and want to retreat. Extroverted people feel more comfortable with these rules, and have more experience testing their boundaries. Introverts spend more time looking within, and lack the skills or habits necessary to push their work out into public. Therefore, to become successful writers, introverts need to extend themselves beyond their comfort zones and learn how to reach toward readers.

The first step is to rationally and logically realize that the rules of social decorum that apply to behavior in public places have little, if any, relationship to the way readers relate to writers.

Readers are free to choose what they read, and will continue to read your works only as long as they remain interested in what you have to say. Empowered by this realization, you can change your image from the embarrassment of standing in a theater of hostile people who wish you would sit down, to the thrill of offering your words to interested readers who desire to read what you have written.

Many writers avoid marketing despite the knowledge that without such effort, their books won't sell. If you still feel reluctant to market yourself, dig deeper into the causes of your own resistance, and challenge the irrational belief that your audience will somehow find you on their own.

Social Restraints Start Early

When I turned five, my scope of movement shrunk to squirming in my classroom chair. For the next 16 years, I sat quietly, and learned that exuberant outbursts earned reprimands. Even now, decades later, when I enter an elevator or an airplane, I withdraw into my own space and make no effort to cross the boundaries that separate me from strangers.

Social training that starts early and is reinforced consistently implants automatic responses in our minds. When one of these automatic thoughts arise, such as "I shouldn't speak loudly here, I might disturb someone" the idea is accompanied by strong emotions, that seem to be arising, not from childhood training, but from some deep, true source. In fact, when social scientists study feelings that govern our behavior toward each other, they see patterns that mimic our instinct for survival.

Such social instincts are observable in the behavior of companion animals. For example, dogs exhibit pack behavior when one, the "alpha," imposes his will on the rest. Horses obey herd behavior, establishing a social hierarchy by nipping, kicking, and posturing. This sense of natural order is built into them, and each horse invests considerable energy seeking and maintaining their place in the hierarchy.

Humans are the most complex herd animal of all. Like some other animals, we live in societies that enable us to protect our young, build shelter, and find food. But humans elevate these social instincts to an art form. We dress, act, and even think like others in order to fit in.

Because our social rules help us survive, violating them creates powerful emotions. Excluding people from the community by shunning, exile, or imprisonment can be one of our severest forms of punishment. At every level of our social life, we aim for approval and fear the consequences of failing to obtain it.

One of the subtlest rules of social life is the general expectation that we will maintain our "proper place." These restrictions seem out of step with modernity, when we are supposed to be able to move up the social ladder any time we want. The emotional readjustment of social climbing is a regular theme in our literature.

One of my favorite classics from British literature, *Great Expectations* by Charles Dickens, is a tale about a poor working-class man who desperately wants to be seen as a "gentleman" to earn the love of a certain young lady. By the end, his upward climb turns out to be based on false premises, destroying his social ambitions.

Many writers feel as if we are embarking on a similar climb. If we transform ourselves into successful writers, we would gain approval and other benefits appropriate to this higher rung. But if we are exposed as imposters, we might be hurled down lower than where we started. Our ambition to seek approval from an audience of strangers awakens social fears with roots deep in our ancestral psyche.

To visualize how such fears might influence your decisions, consider this study conducted in 2003 by Matthew D. Lieberman at the University of California at Los Angeles:

Researchers set up a lab experiment in which they could peer into a volunteer's brain. During the study, the volunteer played a video game in which several people tossed a ball back and forth. When the other ball players stopped tossing the ball to the test subject, he or she reported a sense of rejection. Using magnetic resonance imaging (MRI), the study demonstrated that even playful social rejection triggers pain centers in the brain. At the same time, the brain images showed stimulation in the same areas that are invoked after physical injury.

Lieberman later said in an interview, "While everyone accepts that physical pain is real, people are tempted to think that social pain is just in their heads." He continued, "But physical and social pain may be more similar than we realized. ... Going back fifty thousand years, social distance from a group could lead to death and it still does for most infant mammals. We may have evolved a sensitivity to anything that would indicate that we're being excluded. This automatic alarm may be a signal for us to reestablish social bonds before harm befalls us."

Another classic study was conducted by researcher Stanley Milgram on the subway in New York City in 1974. Milgram instructed his graduate students to ask subway passengers to stand up. The original intent of the experiment was to see how many commuters would comply with this strange request. But the experiment took an unexpected turn. Many of the students froze in terror. Unable to force themselves to make the request, the students felt physically ill, demonstrating the enormous power of social rules. The volunteers themselves became the subjects of the experiment, which shifted its emphasis to looking more closely at the intense emotions aroused by trying to break simple social rules.

Sociological insight may seem irrelevant to writing. But we don't need scientific research to detect the sweaty palms, dry mouth, and agitated stomach before a first pitch to an agent, or the sinking feeling of opening a rejection letter. These mental and physical responses feel similar to those caused by life-threatening danger. The discomfort convinces many of us to avoid public exposure, removing us from danger, but also limiting our options.

Procrastination Protects You from Rejection

A woman came to my workshop insisting that even though she loves writing, she would never be able to write for an audience. I asked her why she had signed up for the workshop if she had no intention of pursuing her desire. After thinking about it, she said, "There's no point in writing, since I'm never going to send out queries." Digging further, she admitted she hates putting herself in the vulnerable position of being rejected. This unspoken anxiety was undermining her ability to write. As soon as she gave it a name, she had a clearer understanding of the hurdle she needed to overcome. Her block had nothing to do with the writing itself, but was caused by her fear of reaching toward strangers.

Procrastination is that peculiar limbo when, despite sincere intentions, you just can't get around to your task. To break its spell, examine the feelings you are attempting to avoid. What danger lurks after you finish your writing project? Might you be afraid your readers will discover you are not "really" an expert, or that you aren't good enough? Naturally fearing such criticism would make the task less attractive. To steer back, create a more optimistic view.

Other, less obvious, fears may be pushing you away, as well. You may fear that your parents are lurking in the background, ready to pounce on you for wasting your time, or some nasty high school teacher wants to remind you of your incompetence.

Among your reasons for shrinking back, you may be shocked to discover the fear of success. If you successfully find readers, you will have to face them. What if you are afraid to look them in the eye? What if you are afraid they will discover it is "only you" behind those flowing words? If you are afraid of your audience for any reason, your fear will slow you down.

Because fear of success seems to make little sense, few of us talk or think about it. Books and classes about marketing and publishing focus on strategies to reach people, rather than on overcoming fear of reaching them. Like other hidden emotions, until you experiment with options, this fear will have the upper hand. For example, you may have always assumed you "can't get around to writing because I don't have enough time." That external cause seems insurmountable.

When you look more closely at your emotions, you might recognize behind your lack of time lurks another problem. Your inaction, at least in part, is not about time but about fear. Once you discover this other reason for procrastination, you ramp up your courage, and discover ways to squeeze writing into the spaces in your schedule. To overcome procrastination, push through fear and look at all your obstacles as puzzles. Then solve them.

Run Toward Readers. Reduce Anxiety. Keep Moving.

When followed, social rules maintain a healthy society. But if we mindlessly obey all the rules, we might be reducing our chances of success. Writers want to go beyond the restrictions that keep us quietly within our private roles. To do so, we must defy our sense of shyness, privacy, or vulnerability.

When you realize how effectively you've been "programmed" to avoid public exposure, you have taken the first step toward changing. Armed with this information, you are empowered to begin your retraining program and develop new responses to carry you toward your dreams.

To prevent the paralysis of procrastination, step back and use the techniques presented throughout this book. Consider the goals you want to achieve. Then use this forward pull to lure you past fears, and start moving.

LOOK TO YOUR AUDIENCE AS IF THEY ARE YOUR FRIENDS

We humans are social beings, as expressed by our attraction toward others, our mutual needs and respect, and pleasure in each other's company. Follow these natural social impulses when you reach toward readers.

REDUCE THE DISTRACTING SENSATIONS OF ANXIETY

By modifying your thoughts and developing a clearer understanding of your emotional sensations, you can shift your focus from the butterflies in your stomach to your creative success.

KEEP MOVING

Use the regular action of your writing habit to overcome procrastination. And when you are ready to reach toward readers, take small, regular steps to defeat the paralysis of inaction.

THOUGHTS THAT INCREASE SOCIAL CONFIDENCE

You can't control your readers' feelings about you. You can't even know them. When you imagine some people in the public won't like you, your discomfort is based on a fantasy about the emotions of people you have never met. Your resulting feelings about imagined critics can tear you down. Such uncomfortable internal conversations drown out thoughts about receptive, supportive readers. To build a trusting relationship with your current and future readers, improve the way you think about them.

Instead of allowing negative thoughts to have their way with you, prepare in advance. Review the thoughts that influence your feelings, and prepare better internal dialogue that can help you achieve your goals. By learning to avoid what psychologists call self-downing thoughts, you can increase your writing energy and enthusiasm.

For example, if you think your audience will respond to your work by pointing their thumbs up or down, you are mistaking them for the crowd's response to Roman gladiators. Such horrible fears naturally detract from your enthusiasm. But with a shift of your fantasy, you can change your audience from enemies to friends. Out of the billions of people who could read your book, many will indeed say, "That's not for me." Those who actually buy your book or read your article are no longer in the thumbs-up or thumbs-down mindset. They want to learn from you, or appreciate what you have to say. Instead of developing a fear-based relationship with them, create one based on trust. Get into the habit of focusing at least as much attention on lurking praise as you do on criticism. Use their curiosity to draw you to them. To increase the energy and creativity of your writing, focus on readers who admire you.

WRITING PROMPT

What disturbing feelings are you creating for yourself by guessing what other people think about your writing? Since you can't read minds, realize that these are your own fantasies, and are neither helpful nor necessarily true. What more positive and reasonable things can you say to yourself that help you feel better about your writing?

EXAMPLES TO HELP YOU REFUTE YOUR NEGATIVE THOUGHTS

Automatic thought:	"He is just pretending to praise my work. He really hates it."
See what you're doing:	I'm mind reading. I'm also "filtering" to see only the worst possible interpretation.

A gentler statement:	"I'll take what he says at face value. If I need more detail, I'll ask. There's no sense making myself miserable by imagining his thoughts."

Automatic thought:	"They don't like me."
See what you're doing:	I'm mind reading. I don't know what they actually think.
A gentler statement:	"I hope they like me."

Automatic thought:	"They don't like me."
See what you're doing:	This is "all-or-nothing" thinking. They like some parts and not others.
A gentler statement:	"It's fun to imagine their positive response to some parts of my writing."

Automatic thought:	"If they don't like it, I'll just die."
See what you're doing:	These catastrophic words make it seem more awful than it is. I know I'll be fine.
A gentler statement:	"No matter what happens, I'll look at it as a step along the way, learn from it, and move to my next challenge."

"Everyone Must Love Me or else I'll Die"

Imagine refusing to appear in front of an audience because you heard there was one person there who might not like you. Such a silly choice makes no sense. Why would you avoid all your fans in order to protect yourself from one person's disapproval? Yet, if you focus too strongly on criticism, you could put yourself in that frame of mind. The demand that every single person must love you grants unreasonable authority to any reader who falls short of total adoration. Shake yourself loose from such extreme expectations by playing around with them.

For example, what if only a hundred million people like you? Would that be good enough? What if out of that hundred million, one of them realized that he didn't like you after all? Would that devastate you or would you be satisfied with the millions who remain?

This impractical idea of universal approval can lead to perfectionism. "If my writing is perfect, then there is no flaw, and no one can find one single thing to criticize." How convenient—a magic formula to get everyone to love you. Real human beings are not that predictable, though. They can fall in love with a frog, or find fault with God. There is no way to please them all.

To think more carefully about expecting everyone to love you, consider your own attitudes toward writers. Your judgment of them is not a simple on-off switch but rather a collection of opinions that varies from work to work, and even differs dramatically within the same piece. Your opinion can change depending on how intrigued you are by the topic, or even how tired you are. Just as your reactions vary wildly, so will your readers. No matter how good your writing, you have no control over all the factors that contribute to their opinions.

Instead of making yourself miserable by longing for the impractical goal of universal acceptance, focus on doing your best. Keep trying, and keep getting better. Seek to understand who you want to please, and then please them as much as possible.

REFUTE FEAR OF CRITICISM WITH AFFIRMATIONS

Even after you pick apart your perfectionism and realize it doesn't make sense, you may still feel driven by perfectionist ideas. To counterbalance these ideas, consciously repeat statements that set the record straight. Here are some affirmations to help combat the draining, demoralizing voice of perfectionism and self-criticism:

- "I choose to write for an audience of caring human beings who will appreciate the enjoyable and informative elements in my work."

- "Kind people don't judge my writing as being 'right' or 'wrong.' They see it as a sincere expression of my creative dreams."

- "There are no 'mistakes' in creativity. My word choices brand this writing with my unique imagination."

- "When I consider all the things I love about other people, I realize how much their uniqueness adds to my pleasure."

- "All humans make mistakes, and if I should happen to make one, it affirms my humanness and unites me with my readers."

- "Each reader will draw conclusions based on his or her own unique preferences and background."

Write affirmations of your own. Keep them handy on 3" x 5" index cards, or post them on the wall or other visible place. Remember that you are a complex individual with flaws mixed with your dreams of contributing to your culture. You just need reminders to lift your sights above the flaws and follow your dreams.

Soften the Fear of Disapproval

In the midst of striving for success, we occasionally find ourselves struggling with our own emotions. We open a rejection letter from an editor or listen to a less-than-enthusiastic comment about our work in a critique group. Often the shock is mild, and we jump back in. *No big deal. I can handle that.* At other times, we feel more vulnerable. Our frustration or other negative emotions distract us from our creative aspirations. In extreme cases, self-doubt could make us want to give up.

When I started to write in my twenties, I went to my first critique group. Someone criticized a single word in one of my poems. I was so hurt, I stayed away from writing groups for thirty years. My inability to accept input prevented me from developing my writing voice.

When I first encountered that terrifying event of someone not agreeing with my word choice, I had no strategies for how to cope with criticism or rejection. Over the intervening years, I developed a repertoire of strategies that have helped me accept and learn from criticism.

I heard an interview with the actor Will Smith who was discussing how he mentally prepared to play the role of the great boxer Muhammad Ali. Smith recounted how as a young man, his mind crumbled when he was hit in the face. He remembered the aha moment when he was first able to receive such a blow, shake off the feelings and keep fighting.

I had a similar aha moment myself. In my fifties, I sat in a critique group sharing a feel-good piece I had written about family harmony. One of the critiquers said in an angry voice, "I hate reading pieces like that." I gulped hard, thanked her for her opinion, and moved on.

Aspiring writers need to do the same–shrug off unsettling emotions–whether because of someone else's criticisms, or because of our own. We take a few deep breaths, set the rejection aside, or smile at the critiquer or rejection letter, and an hour or a day later, we tell ourselves this is just a tiny setback on a long and glorious road. Unfortunately, in a vulnerable moment, we may linger too long on such misgivings and decide writing is not our thing. If the discomfort of criticism or rejection stops you from becoming successful, then learning to cope with these emotions is an important step on your journey.

Prepare to Cushion the Anxiety of Rejection

When you write a query to an agent or editor, you are asking for attention, appreciation, and acceptance. These requests put you in a vulnerable position, and if you receive a "No, that's not for me" response, you could feel rejected. The reality, even for fabulously successful writers, is that rejections are a normal step along the road. If you take rejection personally, you might give up and fade away. To cope with such feelings, develop a more resilient relationship with the submission process.

To find your own way to cope, don't wait until you are in the grip of confusing emotions. Find personal strengths now when you feel comfortable and in control. Developing the beliefs and phrases you want to say to yourself is a very personal and intimate experience, during which you find your own strength and inspiration, whether in religious sayings, in inspirational quotes, in encouraging statements supporters have made to you over the years, or other things you have said to yourself that give you strength.

The first step is to shatter the illusion that someone outside yourself is imposing this pain on you. The truth is, shame and self-doubt turn you against yourself. You are the attacker, not "them." Once you claim ownership of this emotion, you can employ a variety of self-help strategies to protect yourself.

Coach Your Thoughts with Strategy Packs

When you feel intimidated by a phone call you must make to an editor, or a public speaking engagement to promote your book, you must push through the excuses your mind presents about why this is a bad idea and how now is not a good time. To refute those thoughts, you need a clear mind. Unfortunately, once negative emotions are stirred up, it's difficult to remember these energizing thoughts. That is why it is best to plan ahead.

Prepare aids that will provide insight when you most need it. On a deck of 3" x 5" index cards, write compelling reasons for proceeding, or encourage yourself to achieve your goal, or specifically refute some predictable negative statements. There are several types of supportive statements you can include in your strategy pack. Give yourself calming advice. Create a positive atmosphere of loving connection with those for whom you are writing. Remind yourself of your goals. Experiment, and find the supportive statements that work for you. Here are some examples of statements written by students in my workshops:

- "Even if I don't succeed, I'll feel good for trying."
- "After I push myself to do it, it will get easier."
- "I'll breathe deeply and relax my shoulders."

- "My stomach is fluttering because I'm excited. That's good."
- "Have fun."

As you move toward the situation that might provoke disturbing thoughts, flip through your deck of cards, and mull over each supportive statement. Your own encouraging thoughts will help you consider the situation in a more positive light, and defend you against automatic negative thoughts. Keep your strategy pack fresh by adding new, positive thoughts when you prepare for a challenge.

Once you realize the benefit of your own positive statements, you can use this method to push through the anxiety that has been preventing you from accomplishing any writing task.

Refute the Power of Your Inner Critic

If someone said, "You have no talent," you might feel outrage or sorrow, frustrated by this pronouncement that tries to rob you of your voice. Unfortunately, many of us heard such statements from teachers and "well-meaning" family members who wanted to "protect" us from embarrassment. Even worse, many of us say things like this to ourselves, creating a barrier to our own progress.

Counterbalance such demoralizing thoughts with positive ones. As an aspiring writer, you simply want to share yourself through words. Create psychic and social space for yourself by asserting your right to write. The more you insist on your right to communicate, the more empowered and confident you'll feel.

Experiment with various strategies to counteract your inner critic. A firm, "Leave me alone!" is a valid rebuttal to anyone who is being rude to you, even your inner or remembered critics. If you prefer a more diplomatic approach, try something like, "Thank you for your opinion, but please soften your tone, and allow me more creative freedom." Or aim for a shared vision, compromising with your inner critic to achieve pride and dignity. "I know you want this writing to be good. But your harsh demands aren't helping. Let's work together to achieve this goal."

Talking back to your inner critic may at first seem strange, but it's no stranger than your own mind or memory attacking you in the first place. If you passively let automatic self-attacks continue, they block you from achieving your goal. Instead, take an active healing part in this internal dialogue.

WRITING PROMPT

What would you say assertively to an imagined figure who tells you not to write? Extend beyond confrontation to include fun, sharing, and creative intention. "I will entertain you." "I am here to share a piece of my soul." "I will focus on the nonjudgmental part of you." "You are just having a bad day. If you weren't so stressed, you would enjoy this more."

Write your statements on index cards. If you feel intimidated by an imagined audience, pull out your self-talk index cards and repeat these assertive statements.

WRITING PROMPT

If you are afraid of criticism, loosen its grip with exaggeration and humor. Imagine being hired to read your story in a bar. You stand behind a chicken-wire cage to protect yourself from the bottles that patrons throw at you.

Use this image as a setting for an imaginary journal entry, in which you ponder the difference between a safe audience and a dangerous one, and the way your fear of disapproval compulsively motivates you to exclude supporters and only let in the critics.

When self-critical thoughts interfere with your progress, repeat your affirmations in a firm, confident voice. Be assertive. Don't let your mind bully you.

MORE METHODS TO REDUCE SOCIAL ANXIETY

When you fear that someone is or might be criticizing you, the sense of danger hurls you into bottom-of-brain thoughts, anxiousfeelings in your stomach, and primal fears of disaster. To keep writing, you want to raise your attention back to the creative parts of your brain. Here are a few more extreme solutions to help you pry your focus away from these inappropriate emergency responses.

Counter Negative Feelings with Positive Memories

When you feel misunderstood, or under attack, you can increase your sense of confidence by remembering incidents when you were praised and supported. By remembering those experiences, you will feel the corresponding boost in self-confidence in the present. Of course, when you're in the thick of bad feelings, it's hard to remember good ones. Maintain a list of positive memory clips, either in writing or in your imagination, and then pull them out of storage when you need them.

To shift your attention from bad feelings to good ones, select a positive scene from memory, and then free-write about the empowered scene in your journal. When you were celebrating a victory and basking in the confidence and pride of accomplishment and praise, you felt great. You breathed easier. Your positive feelings kept you floating easily above disturbing feelings in your body. Let the memory of those positive feelings radiate through your body now. As you breathe more deeply, soften your eyes. Allow the vitality to flow in your chest. Relax the muscles in your head.

Here's another way to use the past to help you in the present: Rearrange the free-written scenes from your journal and place them in order along a timeline. Gradually, the sequence of your own story will emerge. By seeing how one period of your life flowed into the next, your own life-journal will demonstrate that difficult setbacks provoke courage and personal development, and that time heals. By seeing how your ups and downs progressed over time, you will gain the ancient wisdom to understand that "this too shall pass."

Shift Body Awareness to Increase Confidence

When you are anxious, your stomach tightens, your palms get sweaty, and your heart rate increases. Your racing heart may itself seem like evidence of danger. These automatic bodily responses further accentuate the fear. "The butterflies in my stomach prove I'm in danger. Run!" Such thoughts stimulate even more bottom-of-brain thinking, leading to predictions of catastrophe. The more importance you attach to these sensations, the worse you feel. Panic attacks are the result of getting caught in this loop.

One way to reduce such negative feelings, could be to stop attending critique groups or stop sending queries. Such avoidance reduces your chances of success. To continue on a successful path, look for better approaches.

You can probably find an example in your life when you pushed through fear. Perhaps it was a first date, a first day in school, or a talk you had to give at the office. After you pushed through the fear, you felt fine. Even more important, by pushing through the fear you achieved a healthy milestone in your life.

Similarly, you can overcome your impulse to avoid writing. Using techniques like journal writing and self-talk, you can gradually disengage your mind from the automatic responses of fear. Instead of obeying the impulse to run away from danger, focus on the joy and challenge of self-expression. "The butterflies in my stomach prove that I'm eager to do my best, and anxious to please my readers." With practice you can respond to these sensations with optimistic, light-hearted thoughts that lift your attention away from edgy feelings, into productive energy.

Another method for relieving anxiety bypasses thoughts and goes straight to the muscular tension. With practice, you can learn to scan your body, find the muscles that are storing tension, and relax them. If you tense up when you are writing or thinking about a deadline, relax your diaphragm, neck and shoulders, and your face.

A common response to tighten your breathing muscles. Tense breathing reduces your oxygen supply, fostering rigid, uncomfortable, and unproductive states of mind. If your mind feels trapped, there's an excellent chance you are breathing shallowly. Relaxing your breathing can relax your mind. To breathe all the way into the bottom of your lungs, place your hand over your upper abdomen. Breathe in, and feel your diaphragm muscle expand. When your stomach muscles and diaphragm are relaxed, you will feel your hand rising and falling, up as you breathe in, and down as you breathe out.

Other muscles also pressure your mind when you're uptight. During a contracted frame of mind, your shoulders and chest collapse. Expanding and relaxing your chest and shoulders will help free your feelings.

The muscles in your intestinal tract are called "involuntary," meaning you don't consciously control them, but they do respond to your mood. If you are feeling upset, your intestines react accordingly. So you can relax your guts by learning to relax you mind. Consciously increase mental images of safety, breathe calmly, and let your mind flow toward the joy of creativity. These conscious efforts reduce the danger signals your brain is sending to your involuntary muscles, helping them relax, too.

Improve Your Feelings with Uplifting Visualization

The images you visualize in your mind's eye also have a profound influence on your feelings. Most of our mental video clips are dished up automatically, and we assume we have no influence over them. With practice, however, we can become aware of these automatic images, and intentionally insert more positive ones.

WRITING PROMPT

What do you see when you imagine an important task? A wall of fire? A bottomless pit? A mountain to climb? What color, shape, and texture is your image? Are there people in your image?

What do you see when you imagine the results of your effort? A stern warning? A critical parent? A kind, encouraging, enthusiastic audience?

Just as you can replace the thoughts that drag you down, you can also learn to replace images. To soothe your emotions and create more strength and confidence, you can learn to adjust your visualization. For example, in your mind's eye, picture:

- A safe place
- Brighter colors
- More light
- A successful, confident image of yourself relaxing after the task
- Supportive, friendly people

Visualization will also help you reduce the negative influence of angry or critical figures in your life. You can talk back to them, forgive them, grow wiser in your understanding of the forces that made them who they are, or replace them with more supportive characters.

Neurolinguistic Programming (NLP) teaches about the potential for changing your mood by resizing the images you see in your mind's eye. According to NLP, large, close, and vivid images have the most impact on emotions, and small, far, and blurry images have the least impact. You can experiment in your own imagination to validate this principle in action.

Say for example, you are trying to remember some important scene in your life. If the images are safe, interesting, and pleasurable, picture yourself watching them in a movie theater with an excellent sound system on a panoramic screen. If the images bother you and you need to create more distance, move to the back of the theater. If you still find them disturbing, walk outside for a moment, and when you return, move to a different room where the images are projected on a small, grainy, black and white television. By adjusting your visualization, you can rise above fears and other bottom-of-brain thinking.

A variation on this visualization exercise comes from the ancient principles of yoga. Yogis associate emotions with energy centers in the body, called *chakras*. With this method, instead of focusing on the images themselves, pay attention to the part of your body that is stirred up. The centers lower in your torso, from the stomach down, are oriented toward protecting the self. The centers in the upper half, from the heart up, are oriented to compassion and transcendence. According to this system, you can counterbalance the downward pull of emotions by consciously focusing your attention on your forehead or the top of your head. This upward shift in attention will help you reduce the power of fear, and emphasize the higher intentions of generosity, compassion, and forgiveness.

Snap Yourself Out of Mental Tunnels

Many people experience tunnel vision when they are delivering a speech or listening to their work critiqued by a group. The expression, "a deer in the headlights" describes the feeling nicely. All around you, everything is black, while something bright is barreling toward you, as if you are trapped in a tunnel without any idea how to escape. Such sensations are so intimidating, many writers would rather be struck by lightning than speak to an audience. This reduces our options and literally restricts our vision.

Here is a simple technique that can help you break out of this tunnel. When you feel such a sense of constriction, relax your eyes, softening your focus so you're not seeing anything in particular. Silently describe things in your peripheral vision. Name the color of the wall. Describe the decorations at the edges of the room. "The walls are white. There's a light switch and a picture of a landscape hanging there." With your soft vision, notice your clothes. Actually think the words. "I'm wearing a blue shirt. My shoes are black. I'm holding a piece of paper in my hand." By associating words to what you see, you activate verbal parts of your brain, helping you snap back into your right mind.

Once you are out of the tunnel, you can use familiar rules of courtesy or assertiveness to extricate yourself from the situation. ("Thank you for that feedback. Let's move on." Or, "Sorry. Could you repeat that?") Later, when you look back on the embarrassment of the incident, you can bolster your courage by reminding yourself of the reasons why you put yourself in this situation in the first place. You are in that group, talking about your writing, because of your desire to achieve a level of excellence and earn readers. These goals are in harmony with your image as a writer, and so, by facing and overcoming the emotional hurdle, you have moved a step closer to your dreams.

ACHIEVE CONFIDENCE IN SMALL STEPS

Learning to play the piano takes time. You start at the beginning, learning finger placement, scales and posture. Then you play simple songs. Over time, you learn the theories about rhythm, volume, and sharps and flats. Eventually, your mastery of small tasks leads to worthy accomplishments. Treat your attempt to reach readers with the same methodical approach. Arrange your goals in a series. Start from where you are and proceed step by step to where you want to go.

Learning confidence in a methodical, stepwise manner is called Systematic Desensitization, because it "desensitizes" you to your fears. You could look at it the other way, and call it Systematic Courage Building. Take small, achievable steps. Once you become comfortable at each level, you move on to the next.

I used this method myself to overcome profound social fears. To overcome my fear of public speaking, I simply followed the gentle, gradual process fostered by Toastmasters International. Their program allows members to face their audiences in tiny, safe steps. If you go through their affordable program, you will come out with a greater understanding of the principles of public speaking, and more importantly, you will increase your comfort with your audience.

I also used a gradual process to learn how to be a writer. As an adult who had mainly written either for myself or for technical projects, my initial forays into expressive writing felt intimidating. By gradually immersing myself in writing groups, then reaching out to publications, and finally developing my writing repertoire, I came to accept the role of writer.

Whether you are trying to publish your first article or start your fourth book, a systematic method can help you break the grip of anxiety and inaction. Achieve your task in tiny steps. The victory of each accomplishment will give you confidence to boost you to the next level.

Systematic Desensitization energizes all parts of your brain. Use the left brain to solve problems and prepare in advance. Use the top of your brain to set goals and become the hero of your own story. Your right brain connects you to your audience. These higher functions reduce the fear emanating from your lower brain, and harness its courage.

WRITING PROMPT

To become more aware of the ups and downs of your writing life, keep a journal in which you describe your emotions after each writing session or attempt to reach out to readers. Note positive feelings such as enthusiasm, desire for excellence, and determination. Also note feelings that hold you back. Ask yourself what thoughts, images, or actions are most likely to stall your progress. Are you concerned about showing someone your writing? Does criticism send you over the edge? When you think about calling an editor, do you run for the hills? By writing about your feelings, you increase your ability to savor the positive ones and counteract the negative.

Small Victories Provide Confidence to Achieve Larger Ones

The first task is to break down your writing goals into manageable steps, small enough so that each one seems doable. You want to maintain enough poise at each step so that you can think clearly and apply your coping strategies without becoming overwhelmed. Each victory builds a base of emotional strength that sustains you as you move forward.

Instead of starting at a national magazine, send a letter to your local paper. Instead of applying for an national competition, start by trying to earn one from your regional writing conference.

To gain the confidence to send out queries, list a few small steps that can take you in that direction. Think of a range of publications, such as newsletters, newspapers, or web publications. Go from trivial to prestigious. Consider a broad range of submissions, all the way from a letter to the editor to a polished, feature-length article.

If you are avoiding finishing your project, you can even break that task into small steps. Ask yourself, "What does finishing mean?" First you need to finish a raw, imperfect draft. Then you need to get feedback from a reader, a paid editor, or a writing partner. Then you need to absorb and apply her suggestions. By achieving each step you can lead yourself forward. If you continue to experience anxiety about finishing, look more closely for emotional conflicts. Is your delay just a ruse to protect you from exposing it to others? Or is it a legitimate concern that you are still learning skills? If so, your next small step is to seek help with the craft. Uncover your fear as honestly as possible and then move in the right direction.

Overcome Fears and Gain Comfort at Each Step

You may feel uneasy creating a list that directs you toward your fear. Your uneasiness is a telltale sign that you are moving in the right direction. Take your time. Brainstorm. Talk about it.

Don't worry about order at first. Randomly grab whatever ideas appear. After your first session, sort it, placing the easiest items first. These are only slightly beyond your comfort zone. Then list tasks with increasing levels of emotional reluctance. Each step should feel a little more difficult than the previous one. If the leap between any two steps is too large, you may feel overwhelmed. Go back to your list and fill in the gap with an intermediate action or item.

Many situations seem impossible to reproduce artificially. You can't know how you will react to an actual invitation to speak at a group until your receive one. You can, however, use your imagination and playfully invent mock situations that help you challenge and overcome the types of edgy feelings you have been avoiding.

During the writing life, each new situation will challenge you to grow into unfamiliar situations. After years of experience, you will know learn to cope with surprises. The following exercises are designed not to chart out your actual situations as a future writer, but rather to teach you how to overcome your resistance to trying:

AN EXAMPLE OF A TASK LIST ORDERED BY RELUCTANCE

Here is an example of such a list of activities centered on the audacity to be seen by strangers.

- Take out an anonymous ad in a local paper that says "Hello to all."
- Start a blog and publish your own piece. Since blogs are free, your first one can be anonymous.
- Send the web address to your close friends.
- Send the web address to your social media groups

Here is a list of activities to increase your confidence when you approach decision makers:

- Write a query to a fictitious editor or agent.
- Mail a query to a fictitious address, and consider the returned letter your first "rejection."
- Gather a list of editors.
- Write a query to a real editor, but don't send it.
- Mail it.
- Phone the editor of a small publication, say a local newspaper, to inquire about writing an article. Or find an informal online newsletter or e-zine, and email an inquiry directly to the editor.
- Set up an appointment and meet the editor of a small publication, such as a local weekly. Propose your article, or pitch a couple of alternatives. Even if the answer is "no," you will gain a sense of accomplishment from the meeting.

- Read a book about writing queries.

- Make an appointment with an agent at a writer's conference, even if you don't yet have a book to sell.

- Email a query to an editor of a large publication

WRITING PROMPT

Write your own list of activities that will take you toward some writing task that you have been avoiding. Include any situation that makes you feel uneasy or afraid. You will need a variety of situations, some only mildly agitating and some so disturbing you have a hard time believing you will ever actually tackle them.

Mental Rehearsal Provides a Laboratory for Progress

You can achieve many steps toward success by imagining them. Mental rehearsal and role-play achieve many of the same psychological benefits as the physical variety. For example, if you fear that you won't be able to handle rejection, mail yourself a rejection letter. Play with the wording. Role-play with a friend. Take the role of the editor and slam the writer with an outrageously rude rejection, or an overly gentle one. Or, as the writer, tell the editor you don't need him. Or take the opposite extreme and shamelessly beg. Playfulness and creativity increase empowerment and reduce fear.

You may not be in a position to practice going to a book signing or a radio interview yet, but you can still gain mastery over such fears by vividly imagining them. The trick is to put yourself into the situation and realize that you are OK. By imagining yourself in this situation, you replace fear of the unknown with images of safety and accomplishment.

This attempt to imagine yourself in a difficult situation will itself require some courage, but this is a noble sort of courage that enables you to develop the solution to your own fears. Because you are constructing this situation in your imagination, aim toward a safe, congenial resolution. To help you relate to and then remember your own strategies, write imaginary scenes in which you gain control over your feelings.

IMAGINE

Imagine yourself at a poetry reading. How big is the room? Are people seated at tables or in rows? Describe the lighting. How many people are in the audience? You are next up, and you are distracted by sweaty palms, a tense neck, and thoughts that move in slow motion. Now in your imagination, script anxiety-reducing strategies. Picture your friends in the audience, warmly smiling, projecting encouragement with their eyes. Repeat phrases to yourself that remind you of your service to the audience. All you want to do is make the next few minutes pleasurable for them. Thoughts about service take the emphasis off your own passive responses and focus attention on your positive regard for them. Consciously send relaxation signals to the tense muscles in your neck, shoulders, and eyes.

When you write the details of this scene, give yourself credit for having taken an important step toward self-soothing and achieving your goals.

Now that you have scripted this scene, rehearse it in your imagination. Feel the feelings and see the sights. When you feel safe and secure in that imagined scene, you have actually taken a positive step in your own psychological reality, turning imagination into a powerful tool that you can apply to your real world. Rehearse this scene over and over, using your anxiety-reducing strategies, until you feel you can enter the scene comfortably, without anxiety. This visualized rehearsal becomes a victory that lets you replace social anxiety with social confidence.

During Practice, Use Positive Self-talk and Other Supports

The key to Systematic Desensitization is to become comfortable at each step before moving to the next one, so be patient, and repeat each step as many times as it takes to gain confidence. Don't try to defeat anxiety altogether. Even pros get butterflies when they reach for a higher challenge than the ones to which they have already become accustomed. Instead of fearing or squelching anxiety, work on reducing its distracting intensity. Here is a list of techniques that can help you ease your way through.

- Reduce body tension by breathing deeply and relaxing muscles in neck, face, shoulders or abdomen.

- Recite positive, encouraging statements. For example, "Once I get over the shock, I will have a lifetime to look back on this victory."

- Don't let automatic word choices undermine your resolve. Talk back firmly to your inner critic.

- Find and absorb praise. Seek it from others, and praise yourself.

- Root out self-destructive beliefs such as "I must be perfect" or "everyone must love me." Explain patiently and firmly to yourself that some core beliefs that you learned in childhood are no longer appropriate.

- As you perform the actions on your list, you will be able to feel the success of achieving what was once intimidating. Through repeated effort and success, retrain your emotions and gain the confidence to keep going. Then proceed to the next step. Drawing on the experience of each victory, your anxiety diminishes as confidence grows.

TO CONQUER FEAR, COMMUNICATE WITH LOVE

Fear is a natural survival tool intended to protect us from danger. But if you are afraid of your readers, the only thing the emotion is protecting you from is success. To succeed, learn to feel warm and welcoming toward strangers. Even though embracing them seems daunting, once you thrust your hand in that fire, instead of burning your flesh, the flames turn into a delightful display of colors.

Readers thank us, ask questions, and anticipate the next article or book with curiosity and even enthusiasm. Their receptivity propels us toward our creative goals. This connection is the ultimate reward, not only of writing but of human existence. Serving readers with respect, turns writing into a labor of love.

As aspiring writers, we challenge ourselves to create beauty and insight so profound that others will line up to drink from our well. Arousing that much interest is no small task. We need more than good sentences and structure. To achieve an emotionally vibrant connection with readers, we must go beyond clear words and strive for inspiring ones.

Writing emanates from the wellspring of our minds, so to improve our writing, we improve ourselves. We keep trying, and eventually, with practice, our inner voice flows. Creating beauty through effort is one of the most sublime achievements on earth. It lets us touch the stars.

Review Your Connection with Your Audience

In your journal, complete the following sentences. Repeat this exercise several times to open a verbal link between your unconscious and conscious intentions.

- Instead of retreating from my audience, I will find these ways to move toward them and connect with them . . .

- To keep in mind ideas that help me feel more confident with readers, I will write sayings and post or otherwise remember them in the following ways . . .

- To enhance the power of praise, I will institute the following habit when someone compliments me . . .

Continue the Journey

WRITERS ARE LIFELONG LEARNERS

How to Become a Heroic Writer teaches the essential skills of a writer. As you proceed in your life-journey, continue to develop these fundamental aspects of yourself. Over time, your whole brain will attune to the growing realization, "I am a writer."

SEE YOURSELF AS A WRITER

Your identity as a hero-writer helps you maintain courage and pursue purpose. Once you see yourself in your own story, you can take advantage of this ancient narrative system to establish your goals and see yourself achieving them.

ACT LIKE A WRITER

A regular writing habit carries you through slumps, and moves you toward your dreams. Use planning and to-do lists to establish and maintain the habit. Dance, stretch, doodle, to engage your brain and keep going.

FEEL LIKE A WRITER

Follow techniques to avoid bottom-of-brain thinking that sucks away your resolution and energy. Talk back, shifting your attention from the fear of failure to the exhilaration of service and engagement.

LOVE LIKE A WRITER

You work hard to please your future readers. Gradually, you learn to direct your words to the ones who are drawn to your writing. Despite the fact that these people are separated from you in both time and space, their interest in your work electrifies your writing mind.

PUBLISH LIKE A WRITER

Readers don't come to find you. Exert effort to move your writing toward them. Even after you do this once, twice, or a hundred times, the journey is not complete. With courage, tenacity, and imagination, continue to learn, grow, and reach readers.

TEACH LIKE A WRITER

After spending years becoming a writer, pass your lessons along so others can join you. Teaching is one of the best ways to learn, and it gives you satisfaction that extends out to your community and inward to enrich your soul.

BUILD HABITS TO SUPPORT YOUR WRITING LIFE

During a recent Olympic season, an interviewer asked a coach how he knows which kids are going to make it. He said the ones who rise to the top have more than technical excellence. "They are willing to manage their daily lives in service of their goals." This applies to writers, too. To succeed, develop more than literary skills. Develop habits that support the attitudes, actions, and self-image of a writer.

CULTIVATE A WRITING HABIT

The most important habit for a writer is a daily writing session. It stirs creativity, maintains momentum and contributes to the quality that your readers will admire and enjoy. Daily writing, like any habit, creates a mood of desire. When you look forward to writing each day, you automatically enter the mental state of a writer.

DRAW INSPIRATION FROM WRITERS AND TEACHERS

Take writing classes, attend writing conferences and join writing groups. In the company of other writers, you can swap tips about the writing life and craft. By associating with them, you feel less isolated, and they renew your courage and focus.

REPLACE DEMORALIZING THOUGHTS WITH MOTIVATIONAL ONES

When you are on the sofa, you might think, "I'm tired. I'll write tomorrow." Such thoughts are uttered by the Muse's archenemy, the anti-Muse, whose sole purpose is to distract you from your goals. Learn to replace these thoughts.

NURTURE MENTAL AND PHYSICAL HEALTH

As a heroic writer, take care of your "instrument." Meditation trains you to listen to your wellspring of creative insight. Exercise supports and energizes your neurons.

LISTEN TO EMOTIONALLY SUPPORTIVE READERS

Instead of writing for judgmental, distant readers, focus on the ones who support you. Supportive readers transform writing from an isolated activity to a social one.

WRITE A MEMOIR

Writing a memoir will teach you the intimate connection between life and story. By casting yourself as the hero of that story, you develop a more adventuresome, tenacious visualization of your journey to become a writer.

CONTINUE TO UNITE YOUR BRAIN

Top of Brain: Become the Conscious Author of Your Story

Joseph Campbell found similarities among the myths at the heart of every civilization. His research into stories helped anthropologists understand the similarities among all cultures. Brian Boyd goes beyond the observation that all civilized people tell stories. According to Boyd, the very existence of those civilizations relies on the ability to tell stories.

By understanding the importance of storytelling, we can turn it into a modern tool for self-development. By writing the story of yourself, you can create a customized guidebook that helps you overcome obstacles and strive toward success. Such a story will maximize your self-understanding and help you clarify your long-term goals.

For further insight into the benefit of crafting your story, read my book *Memoir Revolution*. In it, I chronicle the rise of interest in the story-of-self. To take advantage of the ancient tool of Story to help you thrive in today's rapidly changing world, gather notes and anecdotes. For further guidance on finding your own story, read my book *Learn to Write Your Memoir*.

Left Brain: Analysis Helps You Learn Skills and Manage Details

Some writing teachers view the left brain as the enemy, urging you to avoid its tendency to pick things apart. Their advice spurs the flow of free-writing. However, to write for readers, you must edit your material. For this you need your left brain. There are other aspects of writing that also benefit from the judicious use of your analytical thinking Rather than rejecting its influence, enlist the left brain's penchant for breaking things into parts.

- To learn a new writing skill, break it into subskills. For example, storytelling requires dialogue, suspense, character development, etc. Practice each one. Gradually through familiarity, each subskill becomes natural and automatic.

- Simplify difficult projects by breaking them into pieces. To write an article, develop an outline, a working title, and a list of key facts. To write a story, sort events along a timeline and list the key motivations of each character. By achieving each small task, you build satisfaction and momentum that helps you move to the next.

- Break the day into units. Attempt difficult tasks during alert times of day, and mundane tasks when you sag. Use a similar strategy to distribute tasks across the week.

- When your intuition isn't producing results, let go of the flow and attempt to resolve detailed issues. This may provide just the recalibration you need. Your analytical skills and your creative ones synergize, creating a more robust system than you could create with either half by itself.

Left-brain tasks, when applied wisely, will not wreck your creativity. On the contrary – once you form habits, you can stop analyzing and turn the reins back to your automatic mind. For example, after you become accustomed to looking up words in a thesaurus, new words jump to mind on their own. After you become accustomed to editing, you will be able to quickly rearrange sentences and paragraphs to match your own authentic voice.

Keep a self-help or how-to book on your reading pile to supply your left brain with useful ideas. See the list at the back of this book for suggestions.

Bottom of Brain: Rise Above Self-protection and Craving

Nature has evolved rapid-fire brain circuits to increase your heart rate at the first sign of danger. The speed and ferocity of these reactions are crucial when you glimpse a saber-tooth tiger behind a bush. Writers rarely flee predators, but nature presses the same self-protective instincts into service at the first signs of rejection. To protect yourself from danger, naturally you want to run the other way. The instinct of self-preservation convinces many would-be writers that submitting work for publication is too dangerous.

To publish, you must learn to rise above this sense of urgency. When those primal instincts convince you to run the other way, engage the powerful story-telling skills of the top of the brain to provide courage. Use the analysis of your left brain to help you find better words to describe your situation. And use connection with your audience, a right-brain skill, to help you realize they are not your enemies. These higher-brain techniques guide you past the false sense of danger.

In addition to repelling you with fear, the bottom of your brain also tempts you with pleasure. These instincts are crucial for survival. So when you postpone your writing session in favor of a few hours on the sofa eating chips and ice cream, your impulse is reinforced by millions of years of evolution. Fortunately, civilized humans have developed techniques to counterbalance the gravity of bottom-of-brain compulsions.

The heroes of stories weigh the pleasures of the moment against success at the end of the journey. Heroes know that each step takes them closer to their higher goals. By casting yourself as a character in such a story, you will realize that by getting off the couch and writing, you sacrifice immediate comfort in exchange for the future pleasure of turning strangers into friends.

Right Brain: Flow Toward Readers

Free-writing taught a generation of writers to allow their words to flow onto the page. Writing that has been unfiltered by the critical mind helps produce faster first drafts in an authentic, spontaneous voice. A second way to combine flow with the best aspects of your whole mind is to imagine that you are talking to energetic, curious readers. When you lean toward them, to explain and entertain, your whole brain springs into action.

To learn the art of writing for readers, join writing clubs at your local library, college, or bookseller. In such groups, writers serve each other by gently, supportively commenting on each other's work. Joining such a group requires courage, because in addition to supporting you, they can criticize. If you feel skittish and want to bolt, apply self-soothing techniques to ride through the agitation. Constructive feedback helps you achieve technical excellence. In addition to improving your craft, critique groups help you grow as a writer. By exposing yourself to a variety of personalities, you gain the psychological skills necessary for relating to an audience of strangers.

To develop even more connection with your future audience, learn to speak to them. When you stand in front of a small group to read your work, tell a story, or teach, you enhance your emotional connection with the faceless people who will someday read your writing. By learning to speak to them now, before your first book signing or public interview, you will further reduce your fear and energize your writing

The next step is to find readers out in the world. Start a blog and post regularly or find small startup publications whose editors are grateful for your contributions. Feedback from your small audience shows you that your writing voice connects you with real people.

Whole Brain

To become a writer, take advantage of the strengths of each part of your brain. Enlist the top-of-brain for story-telling assistance; recruit analytical thinking from the left brain to plan the next step; follow the all-embracing vision of the right brain to feel the social pleasure of reaching toward readers. By paying attention to input from the three upper parts, you can convince the bottom of your brain that writing a book is the safest and most pleasurable thing you could possibly do with your time.

Even after you successfully reach a plateau, continually improve your whole brain. Apply as much diligent effort to refining your mental skills as you apply to your craft.

THE ROAD AHEAD

On your journey toward becoming a writer, you must overcome the challenges at each stage. Initially, you may think that all you need to do is to clearly express what's on your mind. As you improve in that area, you move on to the next stage in your development. Over time, you discover that verbalizing your meaning is only the beginning. You must go beyond clarity to artfully appeal to readers' imaginations, blazing new trails, surprising, and delighting.

Writers are artists, orators, philosophers, storytellers and even salespersons, as they persuade others to shift from their points of view to yours. What started as a lonely task opens you up to others. Instead of fearing exposure to your audience, you embrace them, seeking to entertain and inform them.

At first you must attempt this feat while sitting alone, addressing an audience that exists only in your imagination. Despite their lack of reality, your mind is on fire, attempting to shape sentences that influence their views of the world. With all your skill you tune your words to appeal to these imagined readers, hoping you will achieve a harmonic resonance, hoping you will read their minds, hoping they will read yours.

To earn your future readers' curiosity, you must maintain an active interest in your own inner life. Writing is like gardening, that near-magical act of creating life from the soil of existence. To reveal insights that connect you with others, challenge yourself to cultivate the vitality of your conscious and unconscious mind.

Socrates said the unexamined life is not worth living. As writers, we have no choice. To succeed we must examine ourselves, our craft, our "instrument" – and so we live a life that *is* worth living.

GLOSSARY OF PSYCHOLOGICAL METHODS

Humanistic Psychology and Talk Therapy: Throughout the twentieth century, talk therapy was one of the main methods for helping people. Talk therapy lets us "use our words" to make more sense of chaotic thoughts and feelings, so we can see past our problems to their solutions.

Logotherapy and Self-actualization: After World War II, Viktor Frankl and Abraham Maslow attempted to help people improve mental health by urging them to focus on a reason for living.

Cognitive Therapy: In the 1950s and 1960s, Albert Ellis and Aaron Beck demonstrated that thoughts affect feelings, and when you improve your thoughts, you improve your feelings.

Neurolinguistic Programming (NLP): In the 1970s, NLP demonstrated that humans learn who they are through training. To change, they need to be retrained. NLP specializes in practical methods for achieving desired states of mind.

Mindfulness Meditation: In the 1980s, psychologist-philosopher Jon Kabat-Zinn brought Buddhism into mainstream medicine by using meditation to help cope with stress-related conditions.

Positive Psychology: In the late 1990s, Martin Seligman launched a branch of psychology devoted to finding ways to improve the human condition.

Neuroplasticity: In the twenty-first century, neuroscientists are taking advantage of the brain's ability to grow. Neuroplasticity fosters strategies for improving brain functioning, in healing from injury (such as stroke), in maximizing potential, and in forestalling decline.

Behavioral Psychology - Habits: Many of us know about the power of habits because of our efforts to stop unwanted ones. As an aspiring writer, you can take advantage of the same research to learn how to start new ones.

FOR FURTHER READING

Civilization has been built upon the recorded words of those who have gone before us. As we ourselves embark on the writer's journey, we can benefit from the abundant resources provided by others with a similar passion. Every author was in the same situation you are in, desiring to write, and then working hard to achieve that dream. Drink of the knowledge, experience, and service that these authors have poured into their writing. They offer their guidance to you. It's there for the taking. Read their words, absorb their messages, and let them inspire you to record your own insights for others to read.

SEVEN HABITS OF HIGHLY EFFECTIVE PEOPLE BY STEPHEN COVEY

This is an inspiring and comprehensive guide to creating an effective, satisfying life. Covey teaches how to create a mission, and then provides a remarkable formula for accomplishing it. This book changed my life by providing me with the simple concept that to achieve goals for myself, I had to apply as much planning and effort as I had previously allocated only to my career.

CHANGING FOR GOOD, A REVOLUTIONARY SIX-STAGE PROGRAM FOR OVERCOMING BAD HABITS AND MOVING YOUR LIFE POSITIVELY FORWARD BY JAMES PROCHASKA, JOHN NORCROSS AND CARLO DICLEMENTE

This book will give you a detailed understanding of how people successfully form or change habits. There is more to forming a habit than "just doing it." In fact, successful self-changers rarely jump straight into the "action stage" without first researching the new behavior, understanding the costs and benefits, and then forming a plan. Even after you start your new behavior, you continue to benefit from strategies that can keep you on track.

THE BRAIN THAT CHANGES ITSELF BY NORMAN DOIDGE

This book provides a thorough background in the new science of neuroplasticity. By appreciating the extent to which you are capable of changing your brain, you can gain an increased trust in the whole project of self-improvement. The book provides a foundation in one of the key scientific revolutions of our time, and can help you visualize the long-term, positive rewards of persistent effort.

EMOTIONAL INTELLIGENCE BY DANIEL GOLEMAN

The massive success of this book helped educate the public about the importance of the limbic system, or the "emotional brain." Dan Goleman created a giant leap in our collective dialogue about the way our emotions influence every aspect of our lives. This book provides an excellent background of the way emotions can rule writing ambitions, and provides insights into how you can regain the upper hand. Additionally, it provides a powerful example of how a book can influence popular thinking.

AWAKEN THE GIANT WITHIN BY TONY ROBBINS

Robbins himself is a giant in the self-help movement. Instead of spending thousands of dollars for his extravagant live performances, read this book. Based on the best of NLP, it is a self-help treasure trove of positive thinking and strategies to get you moving.

MAN'S SEARCH FOR MEANING BY VIKTOR FRANKL

When we read a good story, we expect the main character to desire a goal, and then strive to achieve it. Frankl shows us that these elements are also needed to live a good life. In this inspiring classic, the author explains that finding meaning in life is a minimum requirement for good health and energy, and can solve many problems.

THE FEELING GOOD HANDBOOK BY DAVID BURNS

This is a classic workbook to help you improve your mood and overcome obstacles by teaching you the basics of clearer, more constructive thinking. There is an excellent 40-page section on overcoming procrastination.

WRITING DOWN THE BONES BY NATALIE GOLDBERG

This classic offers insights and exercises to help you get past your inner critic and get in touch with the inner writer. Free-writing sounds easy, but it takes practice. Once you've mastered this technique, it can provide a sound skill set to improve first drafts in any writing task.

THE ARTIST'S WAY BY JULIA CAMERON

This classic workbook gives you exercises and encouragement to energize your creative side. The book cover says it best:

"*The Artist's Way* is an empowering book for aspiring and working artists. With the basic principle that creative expression is the natural direction of life, the author leads you through a comprehensive twelve-week program to recover your creativity from a variety of blocks, including limiting beliefs, fear, self-sabotage, jealousy, guilt, addictions, and other inhibiting forces, replacing them with artistic confidence and productivity.

The Artist's Way links creativity to spirituality by showing in nondenominational terms how to tap into the higher power that connects human creativity with the creative energies of the universe, and guides you through a variety of highly effective exercises and activities that spur imagination and capture new ideas."

THE WAR OF ART, WINNING THE INNER CREATIVE BATTLE BY STEVEN PRESSFIELD

This book is oriented to help writers overcome writer's block. It is motivational, insightful, and instructive. Pressman does a great job of portraying the writing life as a battle to overcome what he calls "resistance." The writing is witty and visceral and takes you inside the author's and by extension, any writer's, heroic struggle to succeed.

STEIN ON WRITING BY SOL STEIN

This book is about writing skills rather than writer's block. I include it here because of the author's ability to portray the mentality of a writer. As you soak up the ideas and attitudes, they enter your being and influence your thoughts. Reading books about writing is a helpful tool for writers.

BIRD BY BIRD, SOME INSTRUCTIONS ON WRITING AND LIFE BY ANNE LAMOTT

This is a wonderful read, and a great insight into the writing life. Lamott offers compassion and insight into one writer's relentless drive to succeed. I consider it "basic reading" for your *How to Become a Heroic Writer* bookshelf.

WRITING PAST DARK, ENVY, FEAR, DISTRACTION, AND OTHER DILEMMAS IN THE WRITER'S LIFE BY BONNIE FRIEDMAN

This is another wonderful read for writers. It is perhaps some of the most interesting prose I have read in years and, like *Bird by Bird,* fills me with joy just knowing I am a human being in the same world where such a book can be written. Keep this and other books about the writing life on your list to give you a strong connection with the complex, inner experience of other writers who struggle with words the way gardeners struggle with plants.

STORY: SUBSTANCE, STRUCTURE, STYLE, AND THE PRINCIPLES OF SCREENWRITING BY ROBERT MCKEE

While the subtitle claims this book is about screenwriting, it actually provides a basis for understanding storytelling in any medium. Even though it is a technical book about the craft, it will provide a foundation that could be valuable for any writer.

Once you recognize the power of stories, you realize they are everywhere. Understanding the nature of stories not only helps you write them, it helps you read them. And it even helps you understand the nature of the human experience, including your own. By fully understanding the role of stories in the human experience, you gain a valuable tool to improve the story you tell about yourself.

WRITING TOGETHER, HOW TO TRANSFORM YOUR WRITING IN A WRITING GROUP BY DAWN DENHAM HAINES, SUSAN NEWCOMER, AND JACQUELINE RAPHAEL

How-to's and anecdotes about forming a creative writing group of your own.

IF YOU WANT TO WRITE: A BOOK ABOUT ART, INDEPENDENCE AND SPIRIT BY BRENDA UELAND

The down-home tone of this book, published in 1938, provides support and encouragement. Gentle and inspiring, Ueland is like the kind mother, mentor, and teacher you always wished you had. According to the author, "Everybody is talented, original, and has something important to say."

WRITER'S JOURNEY, MYTHIC STRUCTURE FOR STORYTELLERS AND SCREENWRITERS BY CHRISTOPHER VOGLER

This book analyzes the story process in the light of Joseph Campbell's *Hero's Journey*, the mythological form found in every culture, in every age. Even if you write nonfiction, if you are interested in the structure of story, this book provides a wealth of information.

ASSERTING YOURSELF, A PRACTICAL GUIDE FOR POSITIVE CHANGE BY SHARON AND GORDON BOWER

Most of us were trained to believe it is impolite to impose our needs on others. Unfortunately, when we take this lack of assertiveness to an extreme, people around us have to read our minds. To improve your relationship with others, and reduce your reliance on their mindreading skills, learn to be more assertive. This skill is especially important for any writer who needs to let the world know you have something to say.

THE ANXIETY AND PHOBIA WORKBOOK: SIMPLE, CONCISE, STEP-BY-STEP DIRECTIONS FOR MASTERY OF: RELAXATION, EXERCISE, COPING WITH PANIC, REAL-LIFE DESENSITIZATION, OVERCOMING NEGATIVE SELF-TALK, CHANGING MISTAKEN BELIEFS, VISUALIZATION, EXPRESSING FEELINGS, ASSERTIVENESS, SELF-ESTEEM, NUTRITION, MEDICATION BY EDMUND J. BOURNE

Your passionate desire can lead to uncertainty, fear of failing, and other anxious emotions. Instead of backing away from your dream, learn to reduce the anxiety. With some training, you can gain the upper hand over these disruptive emotions. Using information from this book and other self-help books on stress-reduction, you can improve your state of mind, and increase the energy you have available for writing.

DYING OF EMBARRASSMENT, HELP FOR SOCIAL ANXIETY AND PHOBIA BY BARBARA G. MARKWAY, PH.D., *ET AL.*

To live together in society, people need to get along, and that means childhood training must impart rules of harmony. One of our lessons is to avoid revealing our private lives in public. Sometimes we take our training so seriously that it holds us back from accomplishing goals that require us to come out into the open.

A person suffering from social anxiety might feel miserable going out on a date, going to the supermarket, or even leaving the house. A writer with social anxiety might tremble at the thought of someone reading our private thoughts. What if you are expected to do book signings or radio interviews? Your willingness to do so could make a big difference in your ability to reach readers.

This book offers a good overview of methods and insights for overcoming reluctance. It does not specifically address the fears and anxieties of writers. If you want to gather all the resources available, the literature of shyness and social anxiety can provide important perspectives.

ONE TO ONE, SELF-UNDERSTANDING THROUGH JOURNAL WRITING BY CHRISTINA BALDWIN.

An excellent technique to polish your voice is journal writing. Free-writing allows you to set aside the "inner critic" and let your words flow. While the process of journaling seems natural and can be self-taught, there are many insights and techniques that can make this work even more effective. Of special interest is the use of journaling for self-discovery. *One to One* by Christina Baldwin is a classic guide to journaling. First published in 1977, it offers insights and inspiration to help you make the most of this invaluable writer's tool.

SIX PILLARS OF SELF-ESTEEM BY NATHANIEL BRANDEN

Self-esteem is one of the key components of the character you have written into the story of your life. Will your character succeed or fail? Do you build yourself up or tear yourself down? This self-help book provides insights and strategies for improving this aspect of your story.

INTRODUCING NEURO-LINGUISTIC PROGRAMMING: PSYCHOLOGICAL SKILLS FOR UNDERSTANDING AND INFLUENCING PEOPLE BY JOSEPH O'CONNER AND JOHN SEYMOUR

This book is a respected introduction to a set of ideas known as Neurolinguistic Programming (NLP). This highly readable book can expand your horizons to include insightful thinking about human nature and how you can change yourself.

THE MIND AND THE BRAIN: NEUROPLASTICITY AND THE POWER OF MENTAL FORCE BY JEFFREY SCHWARTZ, WITH SHARON BEGLEY

This book offers a simple yet powerful strategy to buffer yourself from automatic thoughts, impulses, and cravings that could lead you toward distraction and procrastination. For a more detailed, technical explanation read Schwartz's book, *You Are Not Your Brain.*

OPENING UP: THE HEALING POWER OF EXPRESSING EMOTIONS BY JAMES W. PENNEBAKER

A pioneer in the field of researching journal writing and turning intuitive wisdom into scientific fact, Pennebaker backs up what journal writers have known for years: Writing in a journal helps you feel better. His research extends the benefit to include physical health.

SOCIAL: WHY OUR BRAINS ARE WIRED TO CONNECT BY MATTHEW LIEBERMAN

Because humans rely on each other, we are born with elaborate pain systems that keep us together and make it uncomfortable when we're uncertain about our place in the group. If you are interested in the brain science behind the intense pain of rejection or fear of rejection, read this book.

FLOURISH: A VISIONARY NEW UNDERSTANDING OF HAPPINESS AND WELL-BEING BY MARTIN SELIGMAN

This comprehensive treatise provides an overview, introduction, and history of the Positive Psychology movement, written by its founder.

THE HOW OF HAPPINESS BY SONIA LYUBOMIRSKY

Lyubomirsky presents an excellent review and exploration of current happiness and Positive Psychology teachings and research.

MINDSIGHT: THE NEW SCIENCE OF PERSONAL TRANSFORMATION BY DAN SIEGEL, M.D.

Dr. Dan Siegel is a popular speaker and author who advocates integrating the whole brain in order to achieve mental health and success. The book is part of the new wave of psychology based on neurological advances, neuroplasticity, and positive psychology.

MY STROKE OF INSIGHT: A BRAIN SCIENTIST'S PERSONAL JOURNEY BY JILL BOLTE TAYLOR

A Harvard-trained brain scientist suffered a severe stroke that destroyed the left half of her brain, giving her a personal experience of living solely on the right side. It took her eight years of rehabilitation to return to normal cognitive functioning. The book combines two important features for the writer's brain. It is an incredible example of the power of effort to help rewire the brain. And it was an in-depth experience of what it felt like to live without a functioning left brain.

ON THE ORIGIN OF STORIES: EVOLUTION, COGNITION, AND FICTION BY BRIAN BOYD

According to Brian Boyd and others in this budding field of the science of Story, humans evolved storytelling in order to help us maintain complex social organizations. Storytelling is a critical aspect of our experience as humans.

QUIET: THE POWER OF INTROVERTS IN A WORLD THAT CAN'T STOP TALKING BY SUSAN CAIN

This book provides an in-depth look at those people who seem to have a genetic disposition to turn within. Introverts need their own space to think. For writers, the tendency is crucial, but then that same preference makes it harder to reach out to readers. Read this book to understand the junction between these two opposing forces.

OTHER REFERENCE ITEMS

To research Light Therapy and Seasonal Affective Disorder (SAD), search the web for: "Seasonal Affective Disorder" Or "Light Therapy" Or "Light boxes."

To learn more about the nature of scientific revolutions, read the classic work by Thomas Kuhn, *The Structure of Scientific Revolutions*. It radically shifted our collective understanding of the way science evolves. In fact, it was so influential in beliefs about science that it was revolutionary in its own right.

For deeper insight into the history of thoughts in psychology, read this article by Robert M. Schwartz, University of Pittsburgh and Western Psychiatric Institute and Clinic. *The Internal Dialog: On the Asymmetry Between Positive and Negative Coping Thoughts*, published in the journal, <u>Cognitive Therapy and Research</u> Vol. 10, No. 6, 1986, pp. 591-605. See this, and other articles by Robert Schwartz at <u>www.cogdyn.com</u>.

ABOUT THE FIRST VERSION OF THIS BOOK

When I first learned about the split between the right and left brains, I hoped that it would help me improve my writing. Suppressing my left brain did help me release the unedited material in my own mind. But when I attempted to write for readers, the split-brain model placed too much emphasis on spontaneity, and offered too little guidance to help me plan and learn. The worst limitation of the right-left split was that it didn't address the confusing emotional challenges of being a writer.

Later I added the top of the brain, the mastermind of the operation. Learning about the bottom of the brain helped me cope with the fears and needs bubbling up from the primal core of my being and that distracted me without mercy. Learning how these four parts worked together, for the first time, provided a model of the brain, which could make me a better writer as well as making me feel more unified.

The metaphor of four directions is built into our collective consciousness. Native American myths use the metaphor of *north, south, east, and west* to indicate the whole world. Echoes of that metaphor arise in expressions such as "the four points of the compass" and "the four corners of the earth."

The ancient Greeks believed in another four-part metaphor. According to them, all matter consisted of the four "elements" – earth, air, fire, and water. In the Middle Ages, alchemists attempted to adjust the balance of the four elements to convert worthless metals into precious gold. In the early 2000s, when I first developed my holistic system for becoming a heroic writer, the metaphor of "four elements" seemed apt, suggesting we could transform ordinary thoughts into golden words to readers. I organized my book along the lines of these four elements, highlighting the importance of story, action, attitude, and audience. That first version of the workbook was called *The Four Elements for Writers.*

Over the intervening ten years, revolutionary advances have increasingly made the brain more accessible. Based on this growing body of knowledge, I lined up the four aspects of self-help for writers along quadrants of the brain. In this updated and revised edition, I have woven the journey of the heroic writer into a narrative, linked together by psychology, self-help, and my desire to encourage you to write. In *How to Become a Heroic Writer*, I offer these insights, gained through a lifetime of discovery, to help you on your journey to achieve your creative goals.

ACKNOWLEDGEMENTS

To thank the giants upon whose shoulders I stand, I am passing on to you those gems they've given me.

Thank you to the wise teachers of human nature in the counseling program at Villanova University, especially Nick Rosa and Steve Weinrach. Author and trainer Joseph O'Connor leapt out of the pages of his excellent book and personally taught me how to apply NLP principles to my journey to become a writer. Stephen Covey's *Seven Habits of Highly Effective People* showed me how to pack the right stuff into my day to make my life more meaningful.

The writing community at the Writers Room in Doylestown, Pennsylvania, inspired, encouraged, and taught me, notably Foster Winans, the man who created and "fostered" the club, and Jonathan Maberry, who reincarnated it into a location-independent armada carrying me and an entire community of aspiring writers across the channel from "I love to write" to "I am a writer."

For the first edition, thanks for reading and editing to Brenda Lange, Karin Rex, Dick Lolla, Kelly Daley, Helen Lerner, Diane O'Connell, and Mike Delvechia. For the revised version, thanks to Kerry Gans, Ruth Littner, Joanne Leva, Shawn Kuhn (Mr. SuzyQ), and Rebecca Valentine.

Thanks to my wife, Janet, whose ongoing love and support makes all this possible, and to Katherine, who helps me tune in to the sound of silence. ... To my friends, whose passion for life keeps me moving in the right direction. … To my mother, who lived so long I had the profoundly satisfying experience of adult friendship. ... And to my brother, Ed, who, being older, stayed one step ahead of me in everything, including death. The message he carved on his tombstone he also left as a living legacy to those who loved him: "Ad astra per aspera," loosely translated means "Through hardships to reach the stars."

Thanks to everyone who reaches for their dreams, for as you aspire, you make the world a better place. Special thanks to every reader of this book who, by allowing me to share my thoughts, gives me the opportunity to serve.

About the Author

Jerry Waxler, M.S., earned a Master's Degree in Counseling Psychology from Villanova University, and then set out to become a writer. Based on his years of experience as a journaler, technical writer, and essayist, and years of research into self-help and therapy systems, he developed a series of workshops for writers. From these beginnings, he mastered the essential insights and strategies writers need to achieve their dreams. Jerry is on the Board of Directors of the Philadelphia Writers Conference and is adjunct faculty of Northampton Community College. He is the author of *Learn to Write Your Memoir, a Step by Step Guide*, and *Memoir Revolution: Write Your Story, Change the World.*

Topics for Study Available in this Book

- Get started as a writer.
- Start and maintain a writing habit.
- What is procrastination and what can you do about it?
- Time management for writers
- Attention deficit or creative appetite? Focus-training for writers
- Affirmations and other motivational self-talk for writers
- Dismantling self-doubts and boosting your confidence
- Use the Hero's Journey to achieve your writing dreams.
- What do readers want from you and what will you give them?
- Persuasion 101. Embrace selling.
- Going public. Connecting with people.
- Rejection sucks. How to push through to victory.

For More Information

For more information about scheduled events, to arrange a class or group, or for hundreds of essays and other resources, visit www.jerrywaxler.com.